A BIBLICAL SPIRITUALITY
OF THE HEART

A BIBLICAL SPIRITUALITY OF THE HEART

Jan G. Bovenmars, MSC

ALBA · HOUSE   NEW · YORK

SOCIETY OF ST. PAUL. 2187 VICTORY BLVD., STATEN ISLAND. NEW YORK 10314

Library of Congress Cataloging-in-Publication Data

Bovenmars, Jan G., 1923-
  A biblical spirituality of the heart / Jan G. Bovenmars.
      p.   cm.
  Includes bibliographical references.
  ISBN 0-8189-0584-0
  1. Heart — Biblical teaching.   2. Heart — Religious aspects-
-Christianity — History of doctrines.   3. Sacred Heart, Devotion to-
-History of doctrines.   I. Title.
  BS680.H416B67   1991
  233'.5 — dc20   91-7738
                                                          CIP

Designed, printed and bound in the United States of
America by the Fathers and Brothers of the
Society of St. Paul, 2187 Victory Boulevard,
Staten Island, New York 10314, as part of their
communications apostolate.

Printing Information:

Current Printing - first digit   1   2   3   4   5   6   7   8   9   10   11   12

Year of Current Printing - first year shown

1991   1992   1993   1994   1995   1996   1997   1998

ACKNOWLEDGMENTS

Excerpts from *The Jerusalem Bible* copyright © 1966 by Darton, Longman & Todd, Ltd. and Doubleday, a division of Bantam, Doubleday, Dell Publishing Group, Inc. Used by permission of the publisher.

Excerpts from *The New Jerusalem Bible* copyright © 1985 by Doubleday, a division of Bantam, Doubleday, Dell Publishing Group, Inc. and Darton, Longman & Todd, Ltd. Used by permission of the publisher.

Excerpts from *A New Heart for a New World* used by permission of St. Paul Publications, Homebush, NSW, Australia.

Excerpts from *With a Human Heart*, E.J. Cuskelly, MSC, ed. used by permission of Chevalier Press, Kensington, NSW, Australia.

Excerpts from *Heart of the Saviour*, J. Stierli, ed. used by permission of Verlag Herder, Hermann Herder Strasse 4, 7800 Freiburg, Breisgau, Germany.

Abbreviations

OLD TESTAMENT

Genesis	Gn	Nehemiah	Ne	Baruch	Ba
Exodus	Ex	Tobit	Tb	Ezekiel	Ezk
Leviticus	Lv	Judith	Jdt	Daniel	Dn
Numbers	Nb	Esther	Est	Hosea	Ho
Deuteronomy	Dt	1 Maccabees	1 M	Joel	Jl
Joshua	Jos	2 Maccabees	2 M	Amos	Am
Judges	Jg	Job	Jb	Obadiah	Ob
Ruth	Rt	Psalms	Ps	Jonah	Jon
1 Samuel	1 S	Proverbs	Pr	Micah	Mi
2 Samuel	2 S	Ecclesiastes	Ec	Nahum	Na
1 Kings	1 K	Song of Songs	Sg	Habakkuk	Hab
2 Kings	2 K	Wisdom	Ws	Zephaniah	Zp
1 Chronicles	1 Ch	Sirach	Si	Haggai	Hg
2 Chronicles	2 Ch	Isaiah	Is	Malachi	Ml
Ezra	Ezr	Jeremiah	Jr	Zechariah	Zc
		Lamentations	Lm		

NEW TESTAMENT

Matthew	Mt	Ephesians	Ep	Hebrews	Heb
Mark	Mk	Philippians	Ph	James	Jm
Luke	Lk	Colossians	Col	1 Peter	1 P
John	Jn	1 Thessalonians	1 Th	2 Peter	2 P
Acts	Ac	2 Thessalonians	2 Th	1 John	1 Jn
Romans	Rm	1 Timothy	1 Tm	2 John	2 Jn
1 Corinthians	1 Cor	2 Timothy	2 Tm	3 John	3 Jn
2 Corinthians	2 Cor	Titus	Tt	Jude	Jude
Galatians	Gal	Philemon	Phm	Revelation	Rv

PREFACE

"Heart" is a keyword in the Bible. Father Jan Bovenmars has chosen a text from the Book of Proverbs as his starting point; one of 1,163 examples of the use of the word in the Bible:

> More than all else, keep watch over your heart,
> since here are the wellsprings of life.
>
> (Pr 4:23)

This text makes clear immediately that, in biblical usage, the word "heart" means more than a bodily organ. The heart is the wellspring of life. It indicates what is present and living in the depths of a person. It refers to the origin of what we feel and think, of what we decide, say and do. The quality of a person depends on the quality of his or her heart.

An attentive reading of the Bible reveals how rich and varied are the meanings it gives to the human heart with all its positive and negative possibilities. For the human heart can harden, remain closed in itself and become the heart of a fool. The Bible warns about the "uncircumcised" heart, the heart of stone.

But God too has a Heart, a Heart that is greater than our hearts. His Heart is open to us, concerned for us. He wants to change our hearts and give us "a heart of flesh." In the writings of the Prophets, the promise of a new heart and a new spirit stand out as a culminating point in God's plan.

After examining Old Testament usage, the author turns his attention to the Heart of Jesus Christ as revealed in the New

Testament. The Lord, gentle and humble of heart, source of living water, invites us to become his disciples, disciples with an open and listening heart, ready to follow him and to share in his love for the Father and for all.

Father Jan Bovenmars' biblical reflection on the heart throws light on the Sacred Heart tradition in the Church in ways which at times may surprise us and which enable us to see more clearly its richness. With a skilled hand the author summarizes the main lines of this tradition throughout the ages and opens up fruitful perspectives for the future.

The author is convincing when he writes of the actuality of a spirituality of the heart inspired by the Heart of our Lord. His study is clearly future orientated. Not without reason, in the final paragraph of his Introduction he dedicates his study to the young people in formation in the more than two hundred congregations and institutes dedicated to the Heart of Christ, hoping that it will help them discover the beauty and relevance of their vocation. Other readers too will be able to deepen their knowledge of this tradition of spirituality by reflection on the contents of this book.

The Vatican Council did not mention "devotion to the Sacred Heart" and some have taken that as a sign that this tradition of spirituality has little or nothing to offer the modern Church. Father Bovenmars draws attention to the fact that the term "heart" is used 119 times in the Council documents: five times in reference to the Heart of Christ, 114 times to our hearts. A renewed spirituality of the heart, as explained in this book, forms part of the Council's program for the Church's mission to the world. The Council has invited us to "a change of heart," especially in the Pastoral Constitution on the Church in the Modern World, *Gaudium et Spes*: a change of heart which will enable us really to share "the joys and the hopes, the griefs and anxieties of the people in this age, especially those who are poor or in any way afflicted."

Together with my confrere Jan Bovenmars, I am deeply convinced that an integral spirituality of the heart inspired by the Heart of Christ, and based soundly in the Scriptures and in a creative tradition, is very much needed today. The language of the heart remains a most effective way of presenting the message of the Gospel to the people. The challenge to build a civilization of love, a civilization of the Heart of Christ, is more than ever relevant. The broken hearts of our time (and their number seems to increase day by day) call more than ever for healing, strength and encouragement to build a more human world, a world patterned on the Heart of Christ.

In the midst of all this, growing numbers are feeling in the depths of their hearts a real hunger for a deeper interior life, as formulated so beautifully in the prayer in the letter to the Ephesians:

"Out of his infinite glory, may (the Father) give you the power through his Spirit for your hidden self to grow strong, so that Christ may live in your hearts through faith, and then, planted in love and built on love, you will with all the saints have strength to grasp the breadth and the length, the height and the depth; until knowing the love of Christ, which is beyond all knowledge, you are filled with the utter fullness of God" (Ep 3:16-19).

Cornelis Braun, MSC
Superior General

CONTENTS

Chapter 4
JESUS' HEART IN THE NEW TESTAMENT

Chapter 5
THE RENEWAL OF OUR HEART
ACCORDING TO THE NEW TESTAMENT

Chapter 6
THE SPIRITUALITY OF THE HEART AND OUR LADY

Chapter 7
THE HEART IN CHRISTIAN TRADITION

INTRODUCTION

"If, in the land of their exile, they turn to their heart. . . ."

(1 K 8:47)

Human life is full of variation. When we are young, we go to school and we look forward to the holidays. Afterwards, we start looking for a job, and when we are lucky enough to find one, we have our work to attend to. There is our family life, our contacts with friends, the media, etc. So many things draw our attention that it is quite possible to live outside ourselves, at the surface, without being truly ourselves. Often we have to get into some kind of personal trouble before we start sorting ourselves out.

What do I really want? What is really good? What should I be doing? As long as we have not asked ourselves such questions, we are drifting along, and our life has no heart yet because we have not yet learned to listen to our own heart. We are still in exile. To live authentically as a person, to become our true selves, we have to draw on those inner resources which God has given us: self-awareness, some light within, our deepest longings, our conscience, our hope. This is what Holy Scripture calls our "heart." In our times we may speak of the core of the person, our inner self, interior life, spiritual life; but also the word "heart" is still frequently used in its deep sense. To quote an example:

> In its penetrating analysis of "the modern world," the
> Second Vatican Council reached that most important
> point of the visible world that is man, by penetrating like

xix

Christ the depth of human consciousness and by making
contact with the inward mystery of man, which in biblical
and non-biblical language is expressed by the word
"heart." Christ, the Redeemer of the world, is the one
who penetrated in a unique and unrepeatable way into the
mystery of man and entered his "heart." (Pope John Paul
II, in *Redemptor Hominis*, AAS 71, 1979, p. 273).

Holy Scripture pays much attention to the mystery of the
human heart: around 1,163 texts in the Bible as a whole use
the term "heart," and it is usually the human heart that is
meant. God takes a special interest in our heart: in his eyes,
the quality of a person depends on the quality of his or her
heart. In the context of the promise of a new exodus, a new
covenant, a new heaven and a new earth, God has spoken of
giving us a new heart and a new spirit. It is important to find out
what this means. In the New Testament we find indications
that God renews our heart by his Son and by his own Spirit.

Throughout the ages, Christians have often looked upon
the Heart of the One whom they have pierced (Jn 19:37). They
felt that the source of the new life was there. The Fathers of the
Church had their vision of the birth of the Church from the side
of the new Adam. In the second millennium the mystics
discovered the love of Jesus' Heart. This mysticism was rich
and beautiful, but the theological expression of this vision was
usually rather poor. Instead of looking at the Heart of the new
Adam as a hidden and deep mystery, eventually his Heart was
taken as an external symbol of love, thus forgetting the deep
biblical meaning of the word. The human heart is hidden and
deep; when we make it an external symbol, like in some
advertisements, we run the risk of becoming superficial. It
may be given to us to come to know the heart of someone, when
he reveals himself to us by what he says or does, but then we
have to be touched by his words or actions. The heart of
someone else cannot be known directly. It is superficial to say
that "heart" means "love"; what goes on in the heart of a person
could be something quite different.

In the Western world we often say that we reason with our

head, and that we feel and love with our heart. This is of course a correct way of speaking, but it is not the complete truth. We also like to quote Pascal: "The heart has its reasons which reason knows nothing of." When speaking along these lines we should rather say that "thinking with the head" refers to a particular kind of thinking. Maybe we do not listen enough to the reasons of the heart. It is good English to say: "In his heart he does not really agree." Then we take "heart" in a deep sense. To refer to some other cultures: it seems that in central Africa "heart" is taken in a sense that comes close to the biblical sense; the same is true of the Upanishads of the Hindus, and of the Koran of the Moslems.

It seems to me that the time has come for a renewal of the theology of Jesus' Heart, and that one dimension of this renewal is the biblical dimension. In the biblical perspective, the theology of Jesus' Heart should not be taken in isolation, but should be seen in its biblical context of the theology of the human heart, of God's plan to renew our world and to give us a new heart. In this context, the richness of the mystery of Jesus' pierced Heart can be discovered in a new way, and the meaning of the renewal of our heart can be more clearly worked out.

In the theology of the Fathers and in medieval mysticism, "heart" was still taken in the biblical sense. The same is true of the French School, to which St. John Eudes and St. Margaret Mary belonged. The Heart of Jesus that ravished the saints was his Heart in a deep sense, even when the external symbol was added; even when they discovered that his Heart was all love. What has begun in *Haurietis Aquas* of Pope Pius XII, the return to the Scriptures and to Tradition, should be carried further, and the "heart" should be taken again in its full, biblical sense. This seems to me to be expected from the biblical renewal of theology and of spirituality, and I know that many look forward to this development.

When I speak of a "spirituality of the heart," I am not reacting against recent emphasis on "structural change" in society. On the contrary I believe that the coming of the Kingdom requires structural change, but it should be emphasized too that structural renewal is not possible without the renewal of our heart. New structures can be introduced democratically only when our hearts are in the process of renewal; otherwise they would have to be imposed by force. Only hearts renewed by the compassion of our Lord can envision a society in which justice dwells. Hence: a new heart for a new world.

Biblical renewal is one dimension, but the spirituality of the heart has other dimensions. If we want a new heart for a new world, we have to listen as well to our own heart and to "the heart of the world," to the deep longings of our time. There is the prayer dimension, the missionary dimension, the pastoral dimension, the social dimension, the dimension of art. In this study I will try to make a contribution to a renewed biblical vision of the "spirituality of the heart," by studying the Scripture texts that use the term "heart." Admittedly there are many other relevant texts: texts about the soul, the spirit, about love and mercy. But the texts about the heart are so many that by themselves they are already a very wide field of investigation, and when put together, they provide a surprising vision of God's plan to renew our hearts.

In this study I quote Scripture according to the translation of the Jerusalem Bible of 1966, with a few corrections in line with the New Jerusalem Bible of 1985. I treat only those texts that use the term "heart" in the original text: "leb" or "lebab" in Hebrew; "kardia" in Greek. When the Jerusalem Bible does not use the term "heart" in the translation, I indicate what the original text says.

The last chapter, "The heart in Christian tradition," traces the use of the term "heart" in post-biblical times, especially in the theology of the Sacred Heart. Since the Middle Ages, the human heart was seen more and more as something to be renewed by the Heart of Christ; this became an explicit theme in the time after Vatican II, because of the great stress of *Gaudium et Spes* on the urgent need of a change of heart. It was this development that occasioned this study.

In preparation for this work I made a study of the Scripture texts in which the term "heart" occurs, dividing them according to the various functions of the heart: the heart as bodily organ or area; as interior in general; as center of the emotions; as center of knowing, remembering, willing; God and the heart. A few of these texts, around five, cannot pass textual criticism, but they should at least be discussed. I decided not to include that study in this book. I have added a table at the end indicating all these texts, including the debatable ones.

This study may well offend the sensitivities of some: the term "heart" refers to such a precious mystery that it should not be used too often. In this study I have sinned against that wise precept, but I hope that this sin will be forgiven because of the nature of the case.

Some have said: Why do you speak of a spirituality of the heart? There is no other spirituality! In a way this is true: all spirituality demands a new heart. "Spiritual" life refers to life in the Holy Spirit, the paschal gift of the pierced Heart. Still it is customary to distinguish different spiritualities; we speak, for example, of the Franciscan spirituality, of a Eucharistic spirituality. Now, we all need the spirit of evangelical poverty; we all need the Eucharist. When we speak of different spiritualities, we speak of forms of Christian spirituality, distinguished by some particular accent. The spirituality of the heart is the Christian spirituality with some special attention for the human heart, finding its center in Jesus' Heart and, ultimately, in the Heart of God.

This study is not meant for specialists; I am not a biblical scholar. But having worked my whole life, up to now, for the formation of seminarians in various countries, for young priests and, occasionally, for sisters in formation, I dedicate this little work to the young people in formation, in the more than two hundred congregations and institutes dedicated to the Heart of Christ, hoping that it will help them to discover the beauty and relevance of their vocation. But since this study does not focus specifically on religious life, I hope that it will be of some help as well to all who are interested in the spirituality of the heart. You may find the first three chapters a bit dry; they summarize what the Old Testament has to say on the human heart and the Heart of God. If you have little time, I suggest that you start with the second article of chapter 3: the promise of the new heart. What follows is the fulfillment of that promise. God's promise still stands! Even though God has given us, as first installment, the Heart of his Son, our hearts are still to be renewed by the living water of which the Heart of Christ is the source. The whole of creation is still groaning to be set free, to share in the freedom of the sons and daughters of God. May we, like St. Paul, whose heart was the Heart of Christ, meet Christ on our way, and share in his mission.

A BIBLICAL SPIRITUALITY
OF THE HEART

THE HEART OF THE WISE ISRAELITE

Wisdom literature uses the term "heart" more often than any other section of the Bible: 403 times. These books, therefore, should give us a good impression of the meaning of the term. Included here are five Hebrew works (Proverbs, Psalms, Job, Ecclesiastes or Qoheleth, and the Song of Songs or Canticle), the book of Wisdom written in Greek, and Ecclesiasticus or Sirach, of which I used the Greek text because we do not have a complete Hebrew text.

Of the 403 texts, five speak of the Heart of God, four of the heart of things, two refer to the heart of Satan, while the remaining 392 texts speak of the human heart. It is this last group that we will study in this chapter.

1. The importance of the human heart

> More than all else, keep watch over your heart,
> since here are the wellsprings of life. (Pr 4:23)

This is a good text to open the study of the human heart, for it expresses the importance of our heart: it is the wellspring of life, so we must keep watch over it. Here we are at the source of our feelings and decisions, of our thinking and of what we want, what we say and do; our external behavior is determined by this interior center. We cannot allow ourselves everything; we must keep watch over our desires, our plans, our decisions,

1

and this is more important than all else. For the quality of the person depends on the quality of the heart.

It is possible to exercise some control over what goes on in our heart. The context does not hint at some kind of "examination of conscience" but rather at being careful in choosing our company: "Turn your back on the mouth that misleads, keep your distance from lips that deceive" (v. 24). The heart can be led astray by lying lips; we should rather meditate on words of wisdom: "keep them deep in your heart" (v. 21). The responsibility of keeping our heart pure and upright implies watching over our contacts and, in our days, over the use of the media. This advice is valid for all times; it is a presupposition for a "spirituality of the heart."

> High though the heavens are, deep the earth,
> there is no fathoming the heart of kings. (Pr 25:3)

We do not know what the king thinks or why he does certain things; that is hidden in his heart. The statement is true of all human hearts: the heart is a mystery. The heavens are high, the earth has depths, but the human heart has unfathomable depths. The wise men of Hezekiah's time knew that, long before "depth-psychology" was developed.

> As no two faces are ever alike,
> unlike, too, are the hearts of men. (Pr 27:19)

Again a typical "mashal," consisting of two lines only, the oldest form of Wisdom literature. Externally, people are different, but interiorly they differ too. Emotionally we react differently, we think differently, we make different plans. That makes it so difficult to know the heart of someone else.

> He who trusts his own *promptings* (lit. "his own heart") is a fool,
> he whose ways are wise will be safe. (Pr 28:26)

The wise person does not trust all inclinations, spontaneous feelings and thoughts, the "first reactions." These must be pondered to make our way of life "wise," and that is the purpose of the lessons of the sages. Impulsive action can be foolish.

These four proverbs together form a good introduction to the study of our theme, for they express the importance of the heart as source of life, its depth, its individual characteristics, and the need to watch its reactions. In some 1,163 texts, Scripture has much to say about the heart. God looks at the heart, and so does the sage.

2. The search for Wisdom

The activity most often linked with the heart in Wisdom literature is knowing: to perceive, to think, to reason, to speak to oneself, to imagine, to remember, and to hear one's conscience. Some 112 texts refer to this function of the heart.

> He shaped for them a mouth and tongue, eyes and ears,
> and gave them a heart to think with. (Si 17:6)

> He put his own light in their hearts,
> to show them the magnificence of his work. (Si 17:8)

These two texts of Jesus, son of Sira, provide a religious context for his teaching about the heart as the center of knowing: God gave us a heart to think with, and the light in our heart is a spark of the divine heart, enabling us to admire the beauty and wisdom of creation. There we can find wisdom, for God "poured her out on all his works, to be with mankind as his gift, and he conveyed her to those who love him" (Si 1:9-10).

Sometimes it is the sage who invites us to search for wisdom:

> My son, *attend to me* (lit. "give me your heart"),
> keep your eyes fixed on my advice. (Pr 23:26)

> Listen to me, my son, and learn knowledge,
> and give your whole *mind* (lit. "heart") to my words.
> (Si 16:24)

At other times it is Wisdom personified inviting us to take advice from her: Proverbs 1:20-33; 8:4-36; Sirach 24.

The pursuit of wisdom, however, is arduous and requires discipline. The following quotation is a prayer of a student of wisdom:

> Who will lay whips to my thoughts,
> and the discipline of wisdom to my heart
> to be merciful to my errors
> and let none of my sins go unchecked . . .? (Si 23:2)

> He who rejects discipline despises his own self;
> he who listens to correction wins discernment. (Pr 15:32)

The formation of our heart, "to obtain heart," to become ourselves, requires discipline, listening, attention. We have to learn "the way." Not to do so is foolish, showing lack of respect for oneself. Therefore:

> Teach us to count how few days we have
> and so gain wisdom of heart. (Ps 90:12)

3. What does the sage study?

We could answer this question with the statement of Ecclesiastes 1:13: "With the help of wisdom *I have been at pains* (lit. "I applied my heart") to study all that is done under heaven." In his book *Wisdom in Israel* (SCM Press 1972), G. von Rad distinguishes various centers and transmitters of the didactic traditions, each with its own field of interest. The art of political counseling at the royal court flourished. Esther 1:13 mentions "wise men who knew the times" (original text); interpreters of royal dreams are mentioned in Daniel 1:17; 2:28. The list of sciences enumerated by the author of Wisdom in 7:17-21 is impressive: astronomy, zoology, demonology, psychology, botany and pharmacy. In the oldest part of the book of Proverbs, chapters 10-29, which is considered to be pre-exilic, we find practical wisdom, not intended for the court. It covers a wide range of topics, from tending one's flock to family relations and relations with God. In due time various centers of learning developed; schools for scribes, for priests, for levites, etc. Sirach 39:1-11 gives us the ideal portrait of a scholar.

> Know your flock's condition well,
> *take good care of* (lit. "direct your heart toward") your herds.
> (Pr 27:23)
> He who tills his land shall have bread and to spare,
> he who chases fantasies *has no sense* (lit. "lacks heart").
> (Pr 12:11)
> The life of the body is a tranquil heart,
> but envy is a cancer in the bones. (Pr 14:30)
>
> A kindly glance gives joy to the heart,
> good news lends strength to the bones. (Pr 15:30)
>
> Yahweh loves the pure in heart,
> friend to the king is the man of gracious speech. (Pr 22:11)
>
> He who obtains *wisdom* (lit. "heart") works for his own good.
> (Pr 19:8)

In the oldest layers of Wisdom literature simple maxims about secular topics prevail; at a later stage the form is more developed and the content becomes more theological. On the one hand, Wisdom is presented as the "master craftsman" (Pr 8:30); on the other hand, Wisdom is identified with the Law, and with the Fear of the Lord.

As "master craftsman," Wisdom played its role in creation, when the Lord "poured her out on all his works" (Si 1:9; compare Si 24). The call of Wisdom to the sage to become her disciple is addressed in the first place from creation; in the order of creation he finds rules, scientific rules, rules for personal conduct, rules for government. The heavens and the earth are telling the glory of God's Wisdom. The fool does not notice it (Pr 1:22-32); his ignorance leads to his death. But "whoever listens to me may live secure" (Pr 1:33). Thus we find in Wisdom literature the basis for the doctrine of St. Paul in Romans 1:20 that also without the law the gentiles can know God, and the will of God, from creation. Wisdom literature speaks of the "discerning heart" that notices connections; the "listening heart" that is attentive to the manifestations of the will of God (1 K 3:9), and, on the other hand, of the fool who lacks heart.

> The fool has no love for reflection,
> but only for airing his *opinion* (lit. "heart"). (Pr 18:2)

Consequently, the fool does not understand the signs of the times: "They know nothing, understand nothing. Their eyes are shut to all seeing, their heart to all reason . . . A man who hankers after ashes has a deluded heart and is led astray" (Is 44:18-20).

Texts about the identification of Wisdom with the Law and with the Fear of God are found in Proverbs and in Sirach:

> Wisdom consists entirely in fearing the Lord,
> and wisdom is entirely constituted by the fulfilling of the Law.
> (Si 19:20)

In Si 1:11-20, Jesus ben Sira says that the fear of the Lord is the beginning of wisdom (v. 14), but also its perfection (v. 16) and crown (v. 18). This is Israel's wisdom in its latest stage: the wise man becomes the scholar of the Law. The impressive discourse of Wisdom in Si 24 concludes in v. 23: "All this is no other than the book of the covenant of the Most High God, the Law that Moses enjoined on us." In this chapter, Sirach makes the synthesis between Wisdom as found in creation and as found in historical revelation. In vv. 25-32 Sirach describes wisdom as living water, like the four streams of paradise. Hence:

> The fear of the Lord will gladden the heart
> giving happiness and joy and long life. (Si 1:12)

> Those who fear the Lord keep their hearts prepared
> and humble themselves in his presence. (Si 2:17)

4. *The role of memory*

It seems to me that in the oldest layers of the Old Testament the role of memory as a function of the heart is not stressed, but starting with Deuteronomy we find an impressive series of texts about the word being written in our heart, about remembering the word and pondering it. To develop this thesis let us start from the book of Proverbs.

Proverbs has six texts about the heart as center of remembering, and all six are found in the first nine chapters, that is in the part that was written last:

Pr 3:3	7:3	To write on the table of the heart;
Pr 3:1	4:21	To keep in the heart;
Pr 6:21		To bind to the heart;
Pr 4:4		To treasure: "Let your heart treasure what I have to say."

In the Psalms I found few texts linking the heart to memory: Ps 77:6, and especially:

I have treasured your promises in my heart (Ps 119:11)
I am forgotten, as good as dead in their heart. (Ps 31:12)

A beautiful text from the Song of Songs:

Set me like a seal on your heart,
like a seal on your arm (Sg 8:6)

The Bridegroom asks his beloved to set him like a seal on her heart, so that she will always remember him. This is the opposite of Ps 31:12 where the psalmist is as good as dead in the hearts of others.

A strong confirmation for my "thesis" comes from the Pentateuch, and I would like to include that here. In the Tetrateuch I found no text at all linking the heart to memory, but in Deuteronomy there are seven remarkable texts on keeping the word: Dt 4:9; 4:39, and especially the following five texts about interiorizing the Law, so typical for Deuteronomy:

> Let these words I urge on you today be written in your heart.
> (Dt 6:6)
> Let these words of mine remain in your heart and in your soul; fasten them on your hand as a sign and on your forehead as a circlet. (Dt 11:18)
>
> And when all these words come true for you, the blessing and the curse I have set before you, if you meditate on them in your heart . . . (Dt 30:1)
>
> No, the Word is very near to you, it is in your mouth and in your heart for your observance. (Dt 30:14)
>
> Take all these words to heart; I call them to witness against you today. (Dt 32:46)

These texts illustrate the important role of memory in the spirituality of the heart. Our Lord said that we must hear the word and *keep* it. The word must be received in a generous heart; it must remain in the heart and we must ponder it in our heart. The word of faith must become "vision," for only then can it guide us. These texts from Deuteronomy reflect the promise of God made in Jeremiah 31:33: "Deep within them I will plant my Law, writing it on their hearts." Isaiah complained: "You never took these things to heart or pondered on their outcome" (Is 47:7).

> But in the country of their exile they will take all this to
>   heart and acknowledge that I am the Lord their God.
> I will give them a heart and an attentive ear.
> They will sing my praises in the country of their exile, they
>   will remember my name. (Ba 2:30)

We can speak about remembering the word as a function of the new heart: keeping the word, but also, as in Baruch's text, about remembering something long forgotten, remembering as part of the process of conversion. In this way the prodigal son reflected during the famine: "How many of my father's paid servants have more food than they want . . ." (Lk 15:17). The return to his father's house started with the return in his heart.

5. *The pure heart*

A few wisdom texts speak about planning and willing in general:

> Man's heart makes the plans,
> Yahweh, however, weighs the motives. (Pr 16:1)
>
> A man's heart plans out his way
> but it is Yahweh who makes his steps secure. (Pr 16:9)
>
> Plans multiply in the human heart,
> but the purpose of Yahweh stands firm. (Pr 19:21)

But usually texts about the heart as the center of willing concern either ethically bad actions, which we will consider elsewhere, or ethically good actions which are the theme of this section.

> Listen, my son, and learn to be wise,
> and guide your heart in the way . . . (Pr 23:19)

In some sense our heart *is* the guide of our life, but here the sage advises us to guide our heart. Even though wisdom is a gift of the heart, it should give guidance to help us find our way of life. It seems that in this translation a word is omitted at the end. The Jerusalem Bible suggests: "In the way of prudence"; others: "in the right way." Anyhow, it is the way indicated by wisdom. We can think here of Psalm 1, the psalm of the two ways:

> For Yahweh takes care of the way the virtuous go,
> but the way of the wicked is doomed. (Ps 1:6)

The wise person finds pleasure in the Law of Yahweh and is like a tree planted by water streams. Wisdom literature illustrates the good way in many texts.

> Yahweh loves the pure in heart,
> friend to the king is the man of gracious speech. (Pr 22:11)

Here we should notice first the antithetic parallelism: Yahweh is concerned with the heart, the king with speech. Yahweh loves the pure in heart, those whose heart is innocent, sincere, undivided; this is basic.

> What man can say, "I have purified my heart,
> I am purified of my sin"? (Pr 20:9)

The purification of the heart is an ongoing process; the "way" is also a "way of purification." Before God, our hearts are far from perfect; we need purification, penance, conversion, cleansing to arrive at purity of heart.

> No, Wisdom will never make its way into a crafty soul.
> (Ws 1:4)
>
> Seek him in simplicity of heart;
> since he is to be found by those who do not put him
> to the test. (Ws 1:1)

Crafty: i.e. skillful at deceiving; its opposite is simplicity. Simplicity implies sincerity, unpretentiousness, not having ulterior purposes; its exact opposite is the "double heart" (Si 1:27).

The ethical dimension is most beautifully described in the Psalms. Some 30 texts link the heart with some ethically good action or quality. Most frequent is the expression "the upright heart":

> God is the shield that protects me,
> he preserves upright hearts. (Ps 7:10)
>
> Light dawns for the virtuous,
> and joy, for upright hearts. (Ps 97:11)

Further in Ps 11:2; 32:11; 36:11; 64:10; 94:15; 119:7; 125:4.

"Purity of heart" is mentioned in three psalms. First in Psalm 24, where it is presented as a condition for intimacy with God:

> Who has the right to climb the mountain of Yahweh,
> who the right to stand in his holy place?
> He whose hands are clean, whose heart is pure,
> whose soul does not pay homage to worthless things.
>
> (Ps 24:3-4)

Psalm 73 mentions the human heart six times; purity of heart twice. The psalm opens with a statement that sounds like a thesis, proved by what follows:

> God is indeed good to Israel,
> the Lord is good to pure hearts. (Ps 73:1)

This psalm is a wisdom psalm, a meditation on whether it is worthwhile to keep one's heart pure. At first sight those who don't keep their heart pure, the wicked, are doing well:

> Look at them, those are the wicked,
> well-off and still getting richer! (Ps 73:12)

So the question arises:

> After all, why should I keep my own heart pure,
> and wash my hands in innocence,
> if you plague me all day long
> and discipline me every morning? (Ps 73:13)

During this reflection it dawned on Asaph, the author of the psalm, that intimacy with God is more important than anything else: "those who abandon you are doomed . . . whereas my joy lies in being close to God" (vv. 27, 28). Verse 26 is an impressive statement of "spirituality of the heart."

> My flesh and my heart are pining away,
> my heart's Rock, my own, God for ever! (Ps 73:26) (NJB)

The human heart can truly rely on God, the Rock of our heart, for God is the wisdom and truth we seek, the goodness we long for; God is the faithful and merciful friend we need, our promise and our hope. The pure of heart will see him.

In Psalm 101 (v. 2) the ideal ruler speaks:

> In my household, I will advance
> in purity of heart;
> I will not let my eyes rest
> on any misconduct.

He keeps "perverted hearts" (v. 4) far from him, and cannot tolerate "proud hearts" (v. 5); thus he hopes to prepare the way for the Messiah, "he who comes" (v. 2).

Close to purity of heart is the single-hearted person:

> Yahweh, teach me your way,
> how to walk beside you faithfully,
> make me single-hearted in fearing your name. (Ps 86:11)

Singleheartedness implies sincerity. All efforts are bundled together, all energy is mustered for one purpose, one's whole heart is directed to God. Thus this idea is related to "wholeheartedness":

> Explain to me how to respect your Law;
> and how to observe it wholeheartedly. (Ps 119:34)

"With all my heart," a frequent expression in Scripture, is found also in Psalm 9:2. This wholeness and singlemindedness is to last, not just for a moment, but constantly. Psalm 112 speaks of the one who fears Yahweh:

> With constant heart, and confidence in Yahweh,
> he need never fear bad news. (Ps 112:7)

> Steadfast in heart he overcomes his fears;
> in the end he will triumph over his enemies. (Ps 112:8)

6. The broken heart

Because there is weakness and malice in our hearts, the way to purity of heart is not easy. King David, a proud hero, had to learn humility by his fall. Israel, called to be God's People, needed the experience of the exile. Suffering is needed to arrive at purity of heart.

Psalm 51, the "Miserere," is an important psalm for the spirituality of the heart. It is presented as a psalm concerning David, asking God to purify him from his sin. It is a moving prayer. David is well aware of his fault; he considers himself a sinner even "from the moment of conception" (v. 5) and he asks to be washed clean.

In this prayer we meet with some expressions that are essential for the spirituality of the heart: brokenness of heart, the prayer for a clean heart. David knows that God loves "sincerity of heart" (v. 6), and he realizes that he cannot obtain this state by himself. Hence he prays:

> God, create a clean heart in me,
> put into me a new and constant spirit,
> do not banish me from your presence,
> do not deprive me of your holy spirit. (Ps 51:10)

The clean heart, the new spirit, is a gift of God, a new creation! Then he arrives at an important prophetic insight: Yahweh is not pleased with sacrifices of bulls and sheep, but rather with the sacrifice of a broken heart:

> Sacrifice gives you no pleasure,
> were I to offer holocaust, you would not have it.
> My sacrifice is this broken spirit,
> you will not scorn this crushed and broken heart.
> (Ps 51:16)

The psalmist realizes that what we have to offer to God is really our heart, a heart that recognizes its sinfulness. This refers to the doctrine of the "spiritual sacrifice" and the "spiritual priesthood" that are to become so important in the New Testament. Here we notice the influence of the great prophets: of Isaiah's critique of external sacrifices, and of Jeremiah's and Ezekiel's promise of the new heart and the new spirit. It is evident that not everybody in Judah was ready for this prophetic renewal. The one who added the last two verses to this psalm (Ps 51:18-19) looks forward again to offering young bulls, when the Temple will be rebuilt.

Two other psalms speak of a broken heart:

> Yahweh is near to the broken-hearted,
> he helps those whose spirit is crushed. (Ps 34:18)

> Yahweh, Restorer of Jerusalem!
> He brought back Israel's exiles,
> healing their broken hearts,
> and binding up their wounds. (Ps 147:3)

Again we feel the influence of the book of Isaiah; Is 61:1 says:

> He has sent me to bring good news to the poor,
> to bind up hearts that are broken.

The exile experience gave rise to the doctrine of the spiritual sacrifice and, I think, in connection with this theme, to the expressions of the "broken heart" and the "crushed spirit." The spirituality of the heart was deepened immensely by the terrible experience of suffering, by that new form of "holocaust" suffered in Babylon. But we are very slow learners. How many times do we have to witness such "Holocausts"?

7. *God and the human heart*

Out of 392 texts about the human heart in Wisdom literature, 111 texts link the human heart to God, in one way or another. Some texts speak of what God does to our heart, while other texts treat the human response.

a. Yahweh's action regarding the human heart

We have quoted above two texts from Sirach stating that God gave us "a heart to think with" (17:6) and that "he put his own light in their hearts" (17:8); this refers to God the Creator of the human heart. The formation of the human heart, however, is a long process, and God continues to play a role in it:

> He who moulds every heart
> and takes note of all men do. (Ps 33:15)

Yahweh moulding our heart, God taking a hand in our personal formation. That is an important insight in God's dealing with us. The word "creating" our heart is found only in connection with the renewal of our heart: "God, create a clean heart in me" (Ps 51:12). The renewal of the heart is part of the moulding, and the moulding is part of the creating.

The process of the moulding of the human heart is complex; it is the object of Yahweh's concern during the whole history of salvation. Here we will only enumerate some activities involved.

— *God knows our hearts*:

> Sheol and perdition lie open to Yahweh;
> how much more the hearts of mankind. (Pr 15:11)

> Would not God have found this out,
> he who knows the secrets of the heart? (Ps 44:21)

> Since God sees into the innermost parts of him,
> truly observes his heart. (Ws 1:6)

> He has fathomed the deep and the heart
> and seen into their devious ways. (Si 42:18)

*— God probes and tests our hearts for the sake of
    purification*:

A crucible for silver, a furnace for gold,
but Yahweh for the testing of hearts. (Pr 17:3)

Test me Yahweh, and probe me,
put me to the trial, loins and heart. (Ps 26:2)

— God judges and weighs our hearts:

A man's conduct may strike him as upright,
Yahweh, however, weighs the heart. (Pr 21:2)

Will you object, "But look, we did not know"?
Has he who weighs the heart no understanding?
he who scans your soul no knowledge?
He himself will repay a man as his deeds deserve. (Pr 24:12)

— God moves the heart:

Like flowing water is the heart of the king in the hands of
Yahweh,
who turns it where he pleases. (Pr 21:1)

Whose hearts he then disposed to hatred of his people
and double-dealing with his servants. (Ps 105:25)

This last verse poses the problem of God and sin, a
frequent theme in Scripture. In what sense did God harden
Pharaoh's heart? See also Job 12:24; 17:4; Ps 81:12. In our
time we distinguish between what God positively wills and
what he allows to happen.

— Yahweh's predilection for the broken-hearted:

Yahweh is near to the broken-hearted
he helps those whose spirit is crushed. (Ps 34:18)

You will not scorn this crushed and broken heart. (Ps 51:17)

Healing their broken hearts
and binding up their wounds. (Ps 147:3)

Relieve the distress of my heart,
free me from my suffering. (Ps 25:17)

— *Others for whom Yahweh has a special love*:

> Yahweh, you listen to the wants of the humble,
> you bring strength to their hearts, you grant them a hearing.
> (Ps 10:17)

> Yahweh loves the pure in heart. (Pr 22:11)

> The Lord is good to pure hearts. (Ps 73:1)

> God is the shield that protects me,
> he preserves upright hearts. (Ps 7:10)

> Do not stop loving those who know you,
> or being righteous to upright hearts. (Ps 36:10)

> Yahweh, be good to the good,
> to those of upright heart. (Ps 125:4)

— *Some other actions of God*:

> Yahweh, you have given more joy to my heart
> than others ever knew, for all their grain and wine. (Ps 4:7)

> The precepts of the Lord are upright
> joy for the heart. (Ps 19:8)

> May he grant you your heart's desire,
> and crown all your plans with success. (Ps 20:4)

> Yahweh . . . make me singlehearted
> in fearing your name. (Ps 86:11)

> He will strengthen your mind (lit. "heart")
> and the wisdom you desire will be granted you. (Si 6:37)

b. The response of the sage

— *Seeking God*:

> My heart has said of you,
> "seek his face." (Ps 27:8)

> Those who seek Yahweh will praise him.
> Long life to their hearts! (Ps 22:26)

> You men, why shut your hearts so long,
> loving delusions, chasing after lies. (Ps 4:2)

> In their hearts they were not true to him,
> they were unfaithful to the covenant. (Ps 78:37)

Do not harden your hearts as at Meribah,
as you did that day at Massah in the wilderness. (Ps 95:8)

I turned to the Lord and entreated him,
with all my heart I said . . . (Ws 8:20)

He (Josiah) set his heart on the Lord. (Si 49:3)

— *Praying to God*:

May the words of my mouth find favor;
    and the whispering of my heart,
in your presence, Yahweh
    my Rock, my Redeemer! (Ps 19:14)

I thank you with all my heart, Lord my God,
I glorify your name for ever (Ps 86:12)

So now, sing with all your heart and voice,
and bless the name of the Lord. (Si 39:35)
He (David) put all his heart into song
out of love for his maker. (Si 47:10)

— *Loving and trusting God*:

Trust wholeheartedly in Yahweh,
put no faith in your own perception. (Pr 3:5)

Unburden your hearts to him,
God is a shelter for us. (Ps 62:9)

My flesh and my heart are pining away,
my heart's Rock, my own, God for ever! (Ps 73:26) (NJB)

But I for my part rely on your love, Yahweh;
let my heart rejoice in your saving help. (Ps 13:5)

Our hearts rejoice in him,
we trust in his holy name. (Ps 33:21)

— *Preparing one's heart*:

Those who fear the Lord keep their hearts prepared
and humble themselves in his presence. (Si 2:17)

The man who fears the Lord bears repentance in his heart.
(Si 21:6)

> Do not be unsubmissive to the fear of the Lord,
> do not practice it with a double heart. (Si 1:28)

— *Joy:*

> Those who fear the Lord:
> rich or poor, they will be glad of heart,
> cheerful of face, whatever the season. (Si 26:4)

Psalm 119

So far I have omitted in this section all references to Psalm 119, because this psalm merits to be treated separately. It is a Wisdom psalm, and it is an imposing monument to the Wisdom movement. Wisdom is seen as incarnated in the Word of the Law and the Prophets. The human heart is mentioned 15 times: 14 times in relation with God or the Word of God. The one other time is v. 70: "Their hearts are gross and fat."

— *What does Yahweh do?*

> I run the way of your commandments,
> since you have set me (lit. "my heart") free. (v. 32)

> Explain to me how to respect your Law
> and how to observe it wholeheartedly. (v. 34)

> Turn my heart to your decrees
> and away from getting money. (v. 36)

> Your decrees are my eternal heritage,
> they are the joy of my heart. (v. 111)

> Your Word is what fills me (lit. "my heart") with dread.
>   (v. 161)

— *Nine texts speak of what the heart of the sage does:*

> How happy those who respect his decrees,
> and seek him with their whole heart. (v. 2)

> I thank you from an upright heart,
> schooled in your rules of righteousness. (v. 7)

> I have sought you with all my heart,
> do not let me stray from your commandments. (v. 10)
>
> I have treasured your promises in my heart,
> since I have no wish to sin against you. (v. 11)
>
> Wholeheartedly I now entreat you,
> take pity on me as you have promised. (v. 58)
>
> Though the arrogant tell foul lies about me,
> I wholeheartedly respect your precepts. (v. 69)
>
> Blameless in your statutes be my heart! (v. 80)
>
> I devote myself (lit. "my heart") to obeying your statutes,
> compensation enough for ever! (v. 112)
>
> Sincere, my call (lit. "I call on you with my whole heart") —
> Yahweh, answer me! (v. 145)

This is the picture of a human heart filled with love of God's Word, treasuring the Word, seeking God sincerely, trying to live the Word, finding its happiness in the Word, thanking God for the Word, proclaiming the Word (v. 46).

8. The pure heart and emotions

Some 90 texts in Wisdom literature link the human heart with emotions. If we would list them all, it would look like a phenomenological description of emotional life. Mentioned most often are joy and sadness, but we find also fear, rage, boldness and courage, sympathy and love, antipathy and hatred, gratitude, etc. I am interested here in the attitude of the sages towards their feelings, and so I select those texts which reflect some psychological insight.

a. Joy and sadness

The pre-exilic section of Proverbs already shows great appreciation of joy, though the sage is aware of the relativity of laughter:

Even in laughter the heart finds sadness
and joy makes way for sorrow. (Pr 14:13)

Glad heart means happy face
where the heart is sad, the spirit is broken. (Pr 15:13)

For the sorrowing every day is evil,
for the joyous heart it is a festival always. (Pr 15:15)

A kindly glance gives joy to the heart,
good news gives strength to the bones. (Pr 15:30)

A glad heart is excellent medicine,
a spirit depressed wastes the bones away. (Pr 17:22)

It is to treat a wound with vinegar
to sing songs to a sorrowing heart. (Pr 25:20)

Fragrant oil gladdens the heart,
Friendship's sweetness comforts the soul. (Pr 27:9)

If widows' hearts rejoiced, that was my doing. (Jb 29:13)

Go, eat your bread with joy
and drink your wine with a glad heart. (Ec 9:7)

The Psalms, being more explicitly prayer, relate joy and gladness often to God: 4:7; 16:9; 19:8; 84:2; 105:3; and:

But I for my part rely on your love, Yahweh,
let my heart rejoice in your saving help.
Let me sing to Yahweh for the goodness he has shown me.
(Ps 13:5)

Our soul awaits Yahweh,
he is our help and shield;
our hearts rejoice in him,
we trust in his holy name. (Ps 33:21)

Sadness, sorrow, and suffering, are expressed in many ways and by various images. In prayer the Lord is asked to bring relief.

Relieve the distress of my heart,
free me from my sufferings. (Ps 25:17)

The insults have broken my heart,
my shame and disgrace are past cure. (Ps 69:20)

> That wretch never thought of being kind,
> but hounded the poor, the needy
> and the brokenhearted to death. (Ps 109:16)

> My heart is like wax,
> melting inside me. (Ps 22:14)

> My heart groans, I moan aloud. (Ps 38:8)

> Reduced to weakness and poverty,
> my heart is sorely tormented (lit. "writhes within me").
> (Ps 109:22)

> My heart aches in my breast,
> death's terrors assail me. (Ps 55:4)

> Every fiber of my heart is broken. (Jb 17:11)

b. *Worry, fear and discouragement; boldness*

> Worry makes a man's heart heavy,
> a kindly word makes it glad. (Pr 12:25)

> Hope deferred makes the heart sick,
> desire fulfilled is a tree of life. (Pr 13:12)

> Be strong, let your heart be bold
> all you who hope in Yahweh. (Ps 31:24)

> From the ends of the earth I call to you,
> with sinking heart. (Ps 61:2)

> My heart shrivelling like scorched grass
> and my appetite has gone. (Ps 102:4)

> Fear when hearing thunder:
> At this my own heart quakes,
> and leaps from its place. (Jb 37:1)

c. *Gratitude*

> With all your heart honor your father,
> never forget the birthpangs of your mother.
> Remember that you owe your birth to them;
> how can you repay them for what they have done for you?
> (Si 7:27-29)

When we look at a text like this, we can say that gratitude is implied here. We must remember what others did for us, and "repay" them. Still, the *term* "gratitude" is not used in the Old Testament regarding people; it is used exclusively with regard to God, often reinforced by "with all my heart":

> I give thanks to Yahweh with all my heart. (Ps 111:1)
>
> I thank you, Yahweh, with all my heart,
> because you have heard what I said. (Ps 138:1)
>
> I give thanks to your name for your love and faithfulness;
> your promise is even greater than your fame. (Ps 138:2)

d. *Other emotions*:

Sexual desire:	Do not covet her beauty in your heart. (Pr 6:25)
Confidence:	Her husband's heart has confidence in her. (Pr 31:11)
Desire:	May he grant you your heart's desire. (Ps 20:4)
Inspiration:	My heart is stirred by a noble theme: I address my poem to the King. (Ps 45:1)
Excitement:	See how passion (lit. "your heart") carries you away. (Jb 15:12)
Hurry:	Do not hastily declare yourself before God. (lit. "Let your heart not be in a hurry to speak before God.") (Ec 5:1)
Needling:	Prick an eye and you will draw a tear, prick a heart and you bring its feelings to light. (Si 22:19)

In Wisdom literature we certainly find some fine psychological insights: the joyous heart for which life is a feast; the influence of a friendly glance; the understanding needed for someone in sorrow; the languor caused by hope deferred. We could speak of a certain "civilization of the heart." In the midst of a history of wars and oppression, cruelty and slavery, God moulded human hearts and laid the foundation for a civilization of love towards which we are called. Wisdom literature puts us on the right track, for it teaches us to stay close to God "who moulds every heart" (Ps 33:15).

CHAPTER TWO

THE HEART OF GOD

Revelation in general speaks of God's heart. Creation reveals his generosity, his wisdom and power. Israel's history reveals him as a God of people, Emmanuel, who desires to enter into covenant with us, to redeem us, to lead us to life. The mission of his Son reveals the universal dimension of his love, the depth of his mercy, his plan to establish the Kingdom.

Some particular themes are especially revealing: Yahweh's "hesed," his faithfulness and mercy, his justice, his promises, etc. But the purpose of this chapter is more limited. Here I want to study merely the texts that mention Yahweh's Heart explicitly, to see what is stated there. They too give us a glimpse of God's Heart.

In the Bible as a whole I count 28 texts that mention Yahweh's Heart: 27 in the Old Testament (plus 2 very doubtful ones) and one text in the New Testament (which is a quotation from the Old Testament).

1. Yahweh's thinking and remembering

His heart is wise, and his strength is great:
who can successfully defy him? (Jb 9:4)

Though the majority of the exegetes think that this verse speaks of the Heart of God, some think that it speaks of the heart of those who defy him. The New Jerusalem Bible translates: "Among the wisest and the hardiest, who then can

successfully defy him?" Grammatically, both translations are
possible. I base myself on the more common translation.

Job knows that we cannot argue against God, that we
cannot challenge God: "How can man be right against God?"
(9:9). With his great power he made all things, and he made
them well, for his Heart is wise. Wisdom literature has much to
say about Wisdom, but here we have the source: the Heart of
God.

Job, however, goes on to say: "Nonetheless, I shall speak
not fearing him . . . I will give free reign to my complaints."
(9:35; 10:1). Then follows a speech full of irony, and so we
meet some ironical remarks about God's Heart.

The first ironical text is about God's intentions, but I will
include it here:

> And then you endowed me with life,
> watched each breath of mine with tender care.
> Yet, after all, you were dissembling (lit. "this you intended
>   in your heart")
> biding your time, I know, to mark if I should sin
> and to let no fault of mine go uncensured. (Jb 10:12-14)

God's care is ironically interpreted as attention to catch
Job in some fault, and this is presented by Job as God's secret
intention, hidden in his Heart. Not an edifying thought, and
very far from what Scripture teaches about God's mercy! In
fact, the author of the book knows better. It was only Job's deep
suffering that made him utter this accusation. In 42:8 the
author presents Job as saying: "I retract all I have said, and in
dust and ashes I repent."

A similar ironical remark about God's Heart is found
already in Job 7:

> What is a man that you should make so much of him (lit.
> "that you should put your heart on him"),
> subjecting him to your scrutiny,
> that morning after morning you should examine him
> and at every instant test him?

Will you never take your eyes off me
long enough for me to swallow my spittle?
Suppose I have sinned, what have I done to you,
you tireless watcher of mankind? (7:17-20)

At first sight, the text "What is man that you should put
your heart on him" looks like a beautiful expression of
Yahweh's loving care. But in the ironical context it is taken to
mean, as in 10:13, that God is scrutinizing Job all the time to
find fault with him. And so Job prays for a little less attention!

It is true that Yahweh's attention and care are ironically
presented here, and misinterpreted by Job. The fact remains
(and the author knows it!) that Yahweh has set his Heart on us,
and this fact requires a better interpretation. The real reason
why God set his Heart on us, pays so much attention to us, is
his salvific will, his saving love, as is evident from Scripture as
a whole. He is the one "who moulds every heart" (Ps 33:15).

Three times Yahweh says:

They have built the high place of Topheth in the Valley of
Benhinnom, to burn their sons and daughters; a thing I
never commanded, a thing that never entered my
thoughts (lit. "my heart"). (Jr 7:31; 19:5; 32:35)

Not only is human sacrifice against God's will; the idea
did not even cross his mind, it never entered his Heart. See the
story of Abraham's sacrifice (Gn 22). The whole idea is foreign
to Yahweh's way of thinking.

The incense you offered in the towns of Judah and in the
streets of Jerusalem, you, your fathers, your kings, your
leaders, and the people of the country — is not this what
Yahweh remembered, what came to his mind (lit. "to his
heart")? (Jr 44:21)

This text refers to the worship of "the Queen of heaven."
In chapter 44 Jeremiah refers to the severe punishment that
has struck. He explains its background in the idolatrous behavior of Israel, and he asks: "Have you forgotten the crimes of

your ancestors . . . your own crimes, the crimes of your own wives, committed in the land of Judah and in the streets of Jerusalem? To this day they have felt no contrition nor fear . . ." (44:9). Israel forgets, but Yahweh does not, as long as there are no signs of conversion. Only after conversion and expiation does Yahweh cast our sins behind his back, and does not call them to mind any more. This is a text about Yahweh's memory.

2. Yahweh's planning and willing

> Yahweh's plans hold good for ever,
> the intentions of his heart from age to age. (Ps 33:11)

Psalm 33 is a hymn of admiration of God's Providence, admiration and praise that well up "from upright hearts." The Hebrew text of this psalm mentions the human heart in v. 15: "he who moulds every heart"; and in v. 22: "our hearts rejoice in him." Verse 15 reveals what Yahweh does for us; v. 22 expresses our grateful response.

Yahweh's Heart is mentioned in v. 11. In opposition to the plans of the nations which are shortsighted and unstable, Yahweh's plans hold good for ever, the intentions of his Heart hold from age to age. This verse expresses the stability and reliability of Yahweh's plans. He is faithful, for his great love is without end. His eye rests on those who fear him, not to find fault with them but "to rescue their souls from death, and keep them alive in famine" (v. 19). This is a reason for confidence: "he is our help and shield" (v. 20), and so "our hearts rejoice in him." The psalm concludes with the prayer: "Yahweh, let your love rest on us, as our hope has rested in you."

> Yahweh smelt the appeasing fragrance and said to himself (lit. "in his heart"):
> "Never again will I curse the earth because of man, because his heart contrives evil from his infancy."
> (Gn 8:21)

The expression "to speak to oneself" (lit. "to say in one's heart") usually refers to thinking, but because of the content of this particular thought I consider it here as referring to planning, to God's will. Because of the wickedness of mankind the earth has been washed clean by the flood. Only a remnant was saved. But God will not take such drastic measures again; he knows of what stuff we are made. He knows the weakness and malice of our heart, and he will not curse the earth because of our sins. He puts the rainbow in the sky as a sign of the covenant he made with Noah, "the covenant between me and the earth" (9:13).

This "cosmic covenant" seems to express Yahweh's commitment to preserve the earth notwithstanding human wickedness; God cares for creation. This does not release us from our responsibility for nature, but is rather a call to manage the earth in line with God's intentions, for we are his stewards.

> For your servant's sake, this dog of yours, you have done so great a thing by revealing this to your servant. (lit. "Because of your word and according to your heart you have done so great a thing . . .")

The New Jerusalem Bible translates:

> Because of your promise and since you were so inclined, you have had the generosity to reveal this to your servant.
> (2 S 7:21; 1 Ch 17:19)

The context is Nathan's great prophecy of Yahweh's plan to build David a House that will always stand secure. Then follows David's humble and grateful prayer to which this verse belongs. David sees this promise as coming from the generosity of Yahweh's Heart. In fact, this revelation became the cornerstone of Israel's messianic expectation. Yahweh's Heart is mentioned in connection with the covenant with Noah and with the promises to Abraham and to David. When the new covenant was sealed, the Heart of God's Son was opened to pour out his generous Spirit on us.

3. The sorrow of Yahweh's heart

> Yahweh regretted having made man on earth,
> and his heart grieved. (Gn 6:6)

In the creation story, Yahweh is presented as being
delighted with the works of his hands: he saw that it was good.
After the creation of the first human couple, he "saw all he had
made, and indeed it was very good" (Gn 1:31). Trouble starts
in the human heart: "Yahweh saw that the wickedness of man
was great on the earth, and that the thoughts in his heart
fashioned nothing but wickedness all day long" (Gn 6:5). It is
then that Yahweh's Heart starts to grieve, so much so that he
regrets having made man on earth. It looks as if the earth would
have been better off without man. When in our times we see
whole areas eroded because forests are cut down, flora and
fauna destroyed, we also get that feeling sometimes! At times it
looks as if the worst disaster for the animal world is the
presence of man. We have been bad stewards.

The sorrow of God is about the wickedness of the human
heart. The text presents this wickedness as having reached a
point that made Yahweh decide to make a new beginning.
These verses introduce the story of the flood, a story of punishment, but also a story of the salvation of a holy remnant.

The God of Israel has a Heart, a Heart that can grieve.
This is an anthropomorphism, but these too can be meaning-
ful. In fact they can be more illuminating than learned discourse about the impassibility of God. The Yahwist presents
God as one who deeply cares about what we do, as personally
touched by our response.

4. Yahweh's anger

> The anger of Yahweh will not turn aside until he has
> performed, and has carried out, the decision of his heart.
> (Jr 23:20 and 30:24)

This is a text about Yahweh's anger, a frequent theme in Scripture; more than 200 passages refer to it. We would not have a complete vision of Yahweh's Heart as presented in Scripture if we were to leave out his anger.

The decision of his Heart mentioned in this text refers to the Babylonian captivity. In chapter 23, Jeremiah reacts against the false prophets, who do not speak out against idolatry.

> Do not listen to what those prophets say: they are deluding you,
> they retail visions of their own (lit. "of their own heart"),
> and not what comes from the mouth of Yahweh:
> to those who reject the word of Yahweh they say,
> "Peace will be yours,"
> and to those who follow the dictates of a hardened heart,
> "No misfortune will touch you." (23:16-17)

Evidently the false prophets do not speak out against sin; they do not refer to the anger of God nor to punishment. Jeremiah is different:

> What have straw and wheat in common?
> it is Yahweh who speaks.
> Does not my word burn like fire
> — it is Yahweh who speaks —
> is it not like a hammer shattering a rock? (Jr 23:28-29)

The God of Jeremiah is a God who passionately loves his people, and who cannot sit back and allow them to go astray. What they do matters to him. He not only invites them back when they go astray, but he lets them experience the consequences of their evil deeds. The purpose of allowing their suffering, however, is not their destruction, but repentance: Yahweh wants them to return to him. Hence punishment itself is an instrument of divine love. The anger-texts are an expression of Yahweh's concern for justice and of his passionate love. God's anger refers to the power of the punishment itself, and to the passion of God who will not allow injustice to go unchecked.

False prophets often do not see this dimension of Yahweh's Heart; history proves them wrong. Punishments do occur, and an important dimension of conversion consists in the acceptance of punishment as a gift of God who still loves us.

> For in my heart was a day of vengeance,
> my year of redemption had come.

Or the translation of the New Jerusalem Bible:

> I have decided on a day of vengeance,
> my year of retribution has come. (Is 63:4)

Isaiah 63:1-6 is an apocalyptic poem on the vengeance of Yahweh on the nations. It is one of the most important "anger passages": God's anger is mentioned twice, in v. 3 and 6; his wrath once, in v. 3; his fury in v. 5 and 6. All alone Yahweh had to punish the nations, nobody supported him. Yahweh is presented here as a grape-harvester.

In John's book of Revelation 19:13 and 15, this text is applied to Christ; see also Rv 14:19-20. Yes, the nations receive their punishment, as Babylon was conquered by Cyrus. Christ had to tread the winepress alone, but the blood that covered him was his own.

Isaiah 63:1-6 must be understood within the general context of the texts on Yahweh's anger: punishment is an instrument of Yahweh's saving love. This poem reminds us of it in v. 1: "It is I, whose word is saving justice, whose power is to save." (NJB) His saving justice extends also to the nations. Though the text speaks of "crushing the peoples" and "shattering them," God's punishment is always "saving justice," aiming at conversion. A little further we read:

> I am coming to gather every nation and every language.
> They will come to witness my glory. I shall give them a
> sign, and send some of their survivors to the nations . . .
> and some of them I will make priests and Levites, says
> Yahweh. (Is 66:18-21)

All this becomes clearer when we look at the fullness of revelation: Christ suffered and died for "the many," that is, for all. Even on the day of vengeance, Yahweh's anger is controlled by his love.

> Yahweh said to Jehu, "Since you have done properly what was pleasing in my sight, and have achieved all I set my heart on against Ahab's family. . . ." (2 K 10:30)

In 1 K 21:17-26, Elijah announces to Ahab how his whole family will be punished for the unspeakable crimes of Ahab himself and of his wife Jezebel. 2 K 9:30-37 tells how Jezebel was killed, and chapter 10 narrates the killing of Ahab's sons. Jehu's actions are approved; Ahab and his family were unworthy of the royal throne.

5. *The victory of love over anger in Yahweh's heart*

> Ephraim, how could I part with you?
> Israel, how could I give you up?
> How could I treat you like Admah,
> or deal with you like Zeboiim?
> My heart recoils from it,
> my whole being trembles at the thought,
> I will not give rein to my fierce anger,
> I will not destroy Ephraim again,
> for I am God, not man:
> I am the Holy One in your midst
> and have no wish to destroy. (Ho 11:8-9)

Chapter 11 of Hosea starts with a gripping description of Yahweh's love for Israel: "When Israel was a child, I loved him. . . . I myself taught Ephraim to walk, I took them in my arms. . . . I led them with reins of kindness, with leading-strings of love" (v. 4). But the response of the Chosen People? Disloyalty! "The more I called them, the further they went from me" (v. 2). Hence Yahweh's sadness, disappointment, anger.

Israel should be punished severely: Assyria will come; "the sword will rage through their towns. . . ."

But anger does not have the last word in Yahweh's Heart; love prevails. Punishment can only be medicinal, aiming at the restoration of the bonds of love. The battle in Yahweh's Heart between anger and faithful love is described in Ho 11:8-9. Lamentations 3:33 affirms that Yahweh does not afflict the human race "from the heart." Here in Ho 11:9, Yahweh says that he has no wish to destroy. God's love is redemptive: Hosea 11 ends with a description of the return of the exiles to the promised land. Hosea 11:8-9 is certainly the most dramatic text about the Heart of God, and it expresses beautifully that love prevails in his Heart.

> Since he has no pleasure in abasing (lit. "He does not
> humiliate from the heart")
> and afflicting the human race. (Lm 3:33)

Punishment is the logical outcome of sin. When we have sinned, we must face the consequences. Still, God does not like to punish; what he likes is communion. What Hosea affirmed with regard to Israel is here affirmed with regard to the human race: God's love extends to all people.

Note that not all afflictions are punishments. The book of Job poses the question forcefully. The sufferings of Job himself were a test of his faithfulness. In late Judaism people reflected on the martyrdom of the Maccabees, whose death was heroic. Their case made it clearer that sufferings can have other causes than personal guilt. Whatever the cause, God takes no pleasure in sufferings.

> It will be my pleasure to bring about their good, and I will
> plant them firmly in this land, with all my heart and soul.
> (Jr 32:41)

These words follow the promise of the new heart and the everlasting covenant. When communion is restored, God bestows his rich blessings on his people, and this he does "with his whole heart and soul." The one time that this expression is applied to God, is in a context of faithfulness and blessing.

6. *The transcendence of Yahweh's heart*

> Though you are a man and not a God,
> you consider yourself the equal of God.
> (lit. "you have equalled your heart with the heart of God.")
> (Ezk 28:2)

> Though you are human, not divine,
> you have allowed yourself to think like God. (NJB)

> Since you consider yourself the equal of God.
> (lit. "Since you have equalled your heart with the heart of God.") (Ezk 28:6)

The ruler of Tyre is reproached for his pride. He has been successful in trading, he has made a fortune; now "your heart has grown proud; you thought: I am a God" (28:2). The context suggests that the "equalling of his heart with the heart of God" refers to the way he thinks about his own cleverness. This reminds us of the first temptation: "you will be like gods, knowing good from evil" (Gn 3:5).

But God's ways are not our ways. "As high as the heavens are above the earth, so far is Yahweh's thinking exalted over human thought" (Is 55:9). Here we can refer to Yahweh's challenging words to Job, spoken from "the heart of the tempest": "Who is this obscuring my designs with his empty-headed words? . . . Where were you when I laid the earth's foundations?" (Jb 38:1ff). Man and woman are images of God, reflections of his glory. But our perfection is very relative, whereas God is infinite Truth and Goodness, for whom our heart was made. If there is one thing clear from Scripture, it is the absolute transcendence of God. The creative wisdom of God's Heart fills the universe (see the beautiful Psalm 139). The faithfulness of his love is our inspiration and support; the depth of his mercy is our salvation. His "anger" should make us realize that sin is terribly serious. If the heart of some other human being is already a mystery to us, how much more the Heart of God? "His ways" are so exalted that we cannot know them without his revelation. Thanks be to God for sending us One who could truthfully say, "I am the way." God's wisdom and love incarnate reveal the Heart of God. And the fullness of revelation surpasses the limitations of the Old Testament.

7. *Yahweh's presence*

> I consecrate this house you have built;
> I place my name there for ever;
> my eyes and my heart shall be always there.
> > (1 K 9:3; 2 Ch 7:16)

The purpose of the covenant between Yahweh and his people is communion. A symbol of this communion is Yahweh's dwelling in the midst of his people, first in the Tent of Meeting, and later in the Temple in Jerusalem.

Yahweh consecrated the Temple by taking possession of it, by dwelling in it. That he places his holy name there refers to the presence of his being under the aspect of communion: he can be called upon. The presence of his eyes and of his Heart qualifies this further; he is consciously there, watching his people and saving them. The "heart" is here the center of awareness, but also of God's covenant love. The presence of the holy name makes us think of presence for the sake of worship. The presence of his Heart expresses availability and care.

8. *Leaders after God's heart*

> Yahweh has searched out a man for himself after his own heart and designated him leader of his people. (1 S 13:14; Ac 13:22)

I will raise up a faithful priest for myself; he shall do
whatever I plan (lit. "whatever is in my heart") and whatever
I desire. (1 S 2:35)

I will give you shepherds after my own heart, and these shall
feed you on knowledge and discretion. (Jr 3:15)

In 1 Samuel, the leaders after God's own Heart are men of
that time: king David and the priest Samuel. They were leaders
who carried out the will of God. The text of Jeremiah belongs to
a passage about Zion in the messianic age. Then the nations
will gather in Jerusalem and will no longer "follow the dictates
of their own stubborn hearts." Then Yahweh will give us the
kind of shepherds he desires, shepherds after his own Heart.
Here we can think of Christ, the Good Shepherd, and also of
those to whom he confided his flock.

These verses offer a program to all leaders; they must lead
the people according to God's plan, and feed them on
knowledge and discretion. They are "raised up" by God,
"searched out," "given" to the people; and they find their
guideline in the Heart of God, not merely in the tablets of
stone.

The gift of holy leaders is another sign of Yahweh's care
for his people; he has promised us this gift. In fact, throughout
the centuries, such leaders have not been lacking.

9. *Three remaining verses*

Let me fetch a little bread and you shall refresh yourselves
(lit. "your hearts") before going further. (Gn 18:5)

In Gn 18:13, the guests of Abraham are referred to as
"Yahweh"; so in some sense we have here a reference to
Yahweh's Heart.

The story of the visit of Yahweh to Abraham, the father of
our faith who worshipped "El Shaddai," is unique: Yahweh
having a meal with Abraham. The "heart" here refers to the

whole person, and the person here seems to be: God incarnate. We can look at it as a foreshadowing of the New Testament, in which God truly loves us with a human Heart.

> Were he to recall his breath,
> to draw his breathing back into himself,
> things of flesh would perish altogether,
> and man would return to dust. (Jb 34:14-15)

"Were he to recall his breath": in this translation the word "heart" is omitted, as most think it should be. The Dutch Willibrord translation has: "Were he to close his heart." If that were the meaning, God's Heart would be presented here as the source of life, a function often ascribed to his breath, as in the second part of this verse. But the translation is too doubtful to build on.

> Choosing David as his servant,
> he took him from the sheepfolds,
> called him from tending ewes in lamb
> to pasture his people Jacob
> and Israel his heritage:
> who did this with unselfish care (lit. "with unblemished heart")
> and led them with a sensitive hand. (Ps 78:70-72)

Some exegetes take the last two lines as referring to Yahweh, but this is not probable: "unblemished" is never directly affirmed of God. I agree with the translation of the Jerusalem Bible.

CHAPTER THREE

THE HEART OF STONE
AND THE HEART OF FLESH

The first chapter of this book opened with:

> More than all else, keep watch over your heart,
> since here are the wellsprings of life. (Pr 4:23)

This verse is a good introduction to the study of the heart of the wise Israelite. But now that we want to study the theme of the human heart and sin, I will use another important text:

> Thoughts are rooted in the heart,
> and this sends out four branches:
> good and evil, life and death,
> and always mistress of them all is the tongue. (Si 37:17)

Here the heart is presented, not only as the source of what is good, of life, but also of what is evil, leading to death. Since the heart, in Scripture, stands not only for willing and for the affective life, but also for consciousness, for conscience, for planning, both good and evil are described as coming from it.

There are many texts in which "heart" means "conscience"; for example Job 27:6: "My conscience (lit. "heart") gives me no cause to blush for my life." A beautiful text that sounds rather modern is Si 37:13:

> Finally, stick to the advice your own heart gives you,
> no one can be truer to you than that;

> since a man's soul often forewarns him better than
> seven watchmen perched on a watchtower.
> And besides all this beg the Most High
> to guide your steps in the truth.

This verse teaches a certain autonomy of our conscience, but at the same time it recommends prayer for light from God; the wise man is aware of his limitations.

In this chapter I speak of the moral dimension of the human heart, but also of its religious dimension, for these two are intertwined in the biblical view. The theme of sin in Scripture is an enormous field, and it is not my purpose to cover that whole area. I am concerned only with those texts of the Old Testament that explicitly link sin to the human heart. But even then the number of texts is quite big. A quick count gave me more than 150 texts in the Old Testament alone. To bring some order into this material, I will treat first the texts that speak of the wickedness of the human heart in a general way; then the texts that are more specific. In a final section I will speak of Yahweh's promise to give us a new heart.

ART. 1   THE HEART OF STONE

A. *General statements about the wickedness of the human heart*

The story of the Flood is introduced with a statement describing the wickedness of the human heart as a disease that has affected all people:

> Yahweh saw that the wickedness of man was great on the
> earth and that the thoughts in his heart fashioned nothing
> but wickedness all day long. (Gn 6:5)

When man was not actually doing something evil externally, it seems he was scheming to do so. But also after the Flood Yahweh "said in his heart":

Never again will I curse the earth because of man,
because his heart contrives evil from his infancy. (Gn 8:21)

So it seems that Noah and his posterity suffered from the
same disease. All is not well with the human heart. Let us now
see how this is treated in Wisdom literature and in the
prophets.

1. *Wisdom literature*

In Wisdom literature we find many relevant texts:

If my feet have wandered from the rightful path,
or if my eyes have led my heart astray. . . . (Jb 31:7)

Sin is often described as originating in the heart. In Job,
the heart is seen rather as the victim of external influences (see
Jb 31:9; 31:27; 12:24; 17:4). Temptation may start from what
we see.

The Psalms have much to say about the wickedness of the
human heart in general. Let us start with a text about the heart
of the Israelites:

For forty years that generation repelled me,
until I said: How unreliable are these people
(lit. "They are a people with an erring heart.")
who refuse to grasp my ways. (Ps 95:10)

"They are a people with an erring heart." Israel was
wandering in the desert, but their hearts were equally wandering, not ready to enter the way of Yahweh. The fact of their
wandering in the desert is used as an image to characterize
their heart: wandering, unable to find the place of rest. This
text is quoted and commented upon in Hebrews 3:10. We
should fix our heart on the Lord.

Some further texts from the Psalms:

"perverted hearts" who must keep their distance from the king.
(101:4)

You men, why shut your hearts so long,
loving delusions, chasing after lies. (4:2)

Their hearts are gross and fat. (119:70)

Malice is in their hearts. (28:3)

The wicked man's oracle is Sin
in the depths of his heart. (36:1)

Had I been guilty in my heart
the Lord would never have heard me. (66:18)

From people plotting evil (lit. "devising evil in their heart")
forever intent on stirring up strife. (140:2)

Let me feel no impulse to do wrong
(lit. "Do not let my heart turn to evil")
to share the godlessness of evil-doers. (141:4)

Proverbs, too, has strong statements about sinful hearts:

Men of depraved heart are abhorrent to Yahweh. (11:20)

Men of depraved heart are held in contempt. (12:8)

The heart of the wicked is of trumpery value. (10:20)

Bitterness is in the heart of a schemer. (12:20)

A heart that weaves wicked plots. (6:18)

The unstable heart is satisfied with its own ways. (14:14)

A glaze applied to an earthen pot;
such are smooth lips and wicked heart. (26:23)

Do not trust him if the man be fair of speech,
since in his heart lurk seven abominations. (26:25)

These texts are general in the sense that they do not speak
of specific crimes. They are not general in the sense that they
apply to all men; Proverbs distinguishes clearly between the
heart of the wise and the wicked heart.

Ecclesiastes is convinced that the human heart is in-
clined to evil:

> Since the sentence on wrong-doing is not carried out at once,
> men's inmost hearts are intent on doing wrong. (8:11)

> The human heart, however, is full of wickedness;
> folly lurks in our hearts throughout our lives,
> until we end among the dead. (9:3) (NJB)

2. The heart of a fool

The opposite of the wise man, in Wisdom literature, is the fool, sometimes referred to as the one "who lacks heart." He not only lacks knowledge, but is deficient also in his moral and religious life. I would like to treat the texts about this topic separately.

The fool does foolish things (Pr 15:21); has no regard for reflection (18:2; 15:7); he should come to his senses (lit. "he should acquire heart") (8:5); he neglects his work (10:21; 24:30).

> The wise man's heart leads him aright,
> the fool's heart leads him astray. (Ec 10:2; see also Ec 10:3)

Qoheleth uses also the expression "shallowness of mind" (lit. "of heart"); the heart can be superficial.

Isaiah has texts about the fool:

> For the fool speaks folly,
> and his heart meditates wickedness
> that he may practice godlessness
> and speak wild words about Yahweh. (Is 32:6)

Second Isaiah speaks of those who "know nothing, understand nothing. Their eyes are shut to all seeing, their heart to reason" (Is 44:18). "They never think in their heart" (44:19). He refers also to some who do not take the punishment of God to heart (42:25; 47:7).

Foolishness reaches its nadir in the denial of the very existence of God: "The fool says in his heart: 'There is no God!' " (Ps 14:1; 53:2).

3. The prophets

The prophets, the conscience of Israel, have the strongest texts about our sinful hearts. By way of introduction, let us quote a few general texts here:

> The heart is more devious than any other thing,
> perverse too: who can pierce its secrets? (Jr 17:9)

> But this people
> has a rebellious, unruly heart;
> they have rebelled — being good at this! (Jr 5:23)

> The sin of Judah is written with an iron pen,
> engraved with a diamond point
> on the tablet of their heart
> and on the horn of their altars,
> as evidence against them. (Jr 17:1)

Jeremiah, the prophet who first conveys to us God's promise that the Law of God will be written on the new heart that God will give us, affirms here that sin is engraved on the tablet of the old heart. The negative picture, sketched here, is of course to be balanced with what we have said in the first chapter about the heart of the wise Israelite.

Jeremiah and Ezekiel use sometimes a truly Jewish expression, "the uncircumcised heart." Ezekiel uses it of the gentiles, but Jeremiah (and Leviticus) also of the Israelites:

> See, the days are coming — it is Yahweh who speaks — when I am going to punish all who are circumcised only in the flesh: Egypt, Judah, the sons of Ammon, Moab, and all the Crop-Heads who live in the desert. For all these nations, and the whole House of Israel too, are uncircumcised at heart. (Jr 9:25)

> The Lord Yahweh says this: No alien, uncircumcised in heart and body, is to enter my sanctuary, none of these aliens living among the Israelites. (Ezk 44:9; see also Ezk 44:7)

Under the influence of these great prophets, I suppose, the expression is used also once in Leviticus:

> I in my turn will set myself against them and take them to the land of their enemies. Then their uncircumcised heart will be humbled, then they will atone for their sins.
>
> (Lv 26:41)

B. Hearts turning away from Yahweh

The greatest sin, that so deeply touches Yahweh's heart, is ejecting Yahweh and turning to idols. This is a constant theme in the Old Testament. It was the great temptation of Israel, as exemplified by the story of the golden calf in Exodus. Besides this greatest sin of idolatry, some further sins against God are mentioned: a divided heart, disobedience, superficial worship.

1. Various offenses against God

> "Perhaps," Job would say, "my sons have sinned and in their hearts affronted God." (Jb 1:5)
>
> Deliberately (lit. "from the heart") challenging God by demanding their favorite food. (Ps 78:18)
>
> Do not be unsubmissive to the fear of the Lord, do not practice it with a double heart. (Si 1:27)
>
> For not having attained the fear of the Lord, and for having a heart full of deceit. (Si 1:30)
>
> Because this people approaches me only in words, honors me only in lip-service while its heart is far from me. (Is 29:13)
>
> Worse than all this: Judah, her faithless sister, has not come back to me in sincerity (lit. "with her whole heart") but only in pretense — it is Yahweh who speaks. (Jr 3:10)

Jeremiah uses many times a very strong expression: "to follow the dictates of one's own stubborn (wicked, evil) heart." He applies it both to Israelites and to gentiles. It refers to the refusal to listen to God, and it implies a certain hardening of the heart.

> But they did not listen, they did not pay attention:
> they followed the dictates of their own evil hearts,
> refused to face me and turned back from me. (Jr 7:24)

> They, however, will say, "What is the use of talking?
> We prefer to do as we please; we mean to behave,
> each of us, as his wicked heart dictates." (Jr 18:12)

Similarly, Jr 9:13; 11:8; 13:10; 16:12. Also Baruch 1:22; 2:8. In the messianic age it will be different:

> When that time comes, Jerusalem shall be called: the Throne of Yahweh; all the nations will gather there in the name of Yahweh and will no longer follow the dictates of their own stubborn hearts. (Jr 3:17)

A few texts from the so-called minor prophets:

> Theirs is no heartfelt cry to me
> when they lament on their beds.
> They gash themselves for the sake of corn and wine,
> yet they rebel against me. (Ho 7:14)

> Their heart is a divided heart;
> very well, they must pay for it:
> Yahweh is going to break their altars down
> and destroy their sacred stones. (Ho 10:2)

In this text the divided heart refers to a form of idolatry: these Israelites combined the worship of Yahweh with the worship of other gods.

> If you do not listen, if you do not find it in your heart to glorify my name, says Yahweh Sabaoth, I will send the curse on you and curse your very blessing. Indeed I have

already cursed it, since there is not a single one of you
who takes this to heart. (Ml 2:2)

2. Idolatry

Idolatry is the very negation of the covenant Yahweh
made with his people at Sinai: "I shall be your God, you shall
be my people." It is the sin against the first commandment:
"You shall have no other gods to rival me." In Deuteronomy,
Moses repeatedly warns his people not to let their hearts be
drawn into worshipping other gods: Dt 27:15; 30:17 and:

> Take care your heart is not seduced, that you do not go
> astray, serving other gods and worshipping them.
>
> (Dt 11:16)

Still, the kings and the people repeatedly fell into this
sin, turning their hearts away from Yahweh. Solomon gave the
bad example:

> When Solomon grew old, his wives swayed his heart to
> other gods. (1 K 11:3)

Similarly, 1 K 11:4; 11:9; 14:8. Jehu, too, "did not follow
the law of Yahweh, the God of Israel, faithfully and
wholeheartedly" (2 K 10:31). And king Rehoboam (2 Ch
12:14): "He did evil, because he had not set his heart on
seeking Yahweh." See also 2 Ch 20:33; 25:2; 2 M 2:3.

The Wisdom books

Job asks himself whether he has let himself be tempted to
worship the sun and the moon:

> Or has the sight of the sun in its glory,
> or the glow of the moon as it walks the sky,
> stolen my heart, so that my hand

> blew them a secret kiss?
> That too would be a criminal offense,
> to have denied the supreme God. (Jb 31:27)

We may look at the worship of the sun or the moon as something primitive. But when in our time people set their hearts on money, or on their own glory, they lose their hearts in fact to lesser things! The most extreme form of irreligion is found in the heart of the fool: "The fool says in his heart, 'There is no God!' " (Ps 14:1; 53:2). Usually Israel did not go that far, but still:

> In their hearts they were not true to him,
> they were unfaithful to the covenant. (Ps 78:37)

Of the enemies of Israel the psalmist says:

> Unanimous in their plot (lit. "They plotted
> in their hearts together"),
> they seal a treaty against you. (Ps 83:5)

This treaty was directed against Israel; but, in the psalmist's view, where the survival of Israel is at stake, God's interests are at stake.

Psalm 10 reflects on the thoughts of the wicked; in this context there are three references to his heart:

> "Nothing can shake me," he assures himself (lit. "he
> says in his heart"). (Ps 10:6)

> He says in his heart, "God forgets,
> he has turned away his face to avoid seeing the end."
> (Ps 10:11) (NJB)

> Why does the wicked man spurn God,
> assuring himself (lit. "saying in his heart"),
> "He will not make me pay"? (Ps 10:13)

We can call this "practical atheism," behaving as if there were no God.

The book of Wisdom says that the heart of the idolater is
worthless:

> Ashes, his heart,
> meaner than dirt his hope,
> his life more ignoble than clay,
> since he misconceives the One who shaped him. (Ws 15:10)

And Ecclesiasticus:

> The beginning of human pride is to desert the Lord,
> and to turn one's heart away from one's maker. (Si 10:12)

The prophets have the most moving texts about idolatry,
about the heart that turns away from Yahweh:

> A man who hankers after ashes has a deluded heart
> and is led astray. He will never free his soul or say,
> "What I have in my hand is nothing but a lie." (Is 44:20)

> Who was it you dreaded, and feared,
> that you should disown me,
> and not remember me,
> and refuse me a place in your heart? (Is 57:11)

> Turning our back on our God,
> talking treachery and revolt,
> murmuring lies in our heart. (Is 59:13)

> Yahweh says this:
> "A curse on the man who puts his trust in man,
> who relies on things of flesh,
> whose heart turns from Yahweh." (Jr 17:5)

Among the prophets, Ezekiel stands out with many strong texts
about the heart that deserts Yahweh: Ezk 6:9; 11:21; 14:3;
14:4; 14:5; 14:7; 20:16.
    To quote some of these:

> Son of man, these people have enshrined their own idols in
> their hearts; they cling to the cause of their sins. (Ezk 14:3)

> And in this way I hope to touch the heart of the House of
> Israel who have deserted me in favor of a pack of idols.
> (Ezk 14:5)

Worst of all is setting oneself up as God; of this Ezekiel accuses the king of Tyre:

> Being swollen with pride,
> you have said: I am a god;
> I am sitting on the throne of God,
> surrounded by the seas (lit. "in the heart of the water").
> Though you are a man and not a god,
> you consider yourself the equal of God
> (lit. "you have equalled your heart to the heart of God").
>
> (Ezk 28:3)

3. The hardened heart

When Yahweh promised to give us a new heart, he said he would take away our heart of stone. The image of the "heart of stone" is appropriate, since Scripture has so many texts about the "hardening of the heart." When treating Jeremiah's expression "to follow the dictates of one's stubborn heart" (ch. 3, B 1), I mentioned that it implies a certain hardening of the heart. But many other texts express the hardening of the heart explicitly, or speak of a "stubborn" or "adamant" heart. Because of the importance of this theme I will now treat these texts in detail.

a. The Pentateuch and the historical books

The classical example of the hardening of heart is the Pharaoh. Exodus alone has 18 texts about his hard or stubborn heart, and the expression is used once of his courtiers and once of "the Egyptians." Eleven times Yahweh is said to harden the Pharaoh's heart (or the heart of the Egyptians): Ex 4:21; 7:3; 9:12; 10:1 (twice); 10:20; 10:27; 11:10; 14:4; 14:8; 14:17. Two examples:

> I myself will harden his heart, and he will not let the people go. (Ex 4:21)

> Then I shall make Pharaoh's heart stubborn and he
> will set out in pursuit of them. (Ex 14:4)

Nine times Pharaoh's heart is said to be stubborn or
adamant (the New Jerusalem Bible uses the term "obstinate"):
Ex 7:13; 7:14; 7:22; 8:11; 8:15; 8:28; 9:7; 9:34; 9:35.
Examples:

> Yet Pharaoh's heart was stubborn and, as Yahweh had
> foretold, he would not listen to Moses and Aaron.
> (Ex 7:13)
> But Pharaoh was adamant this time too and did not let the
> people go (lit. "But the heart of Pharaoh was ada-
> mant . . .") (Ex 8:28)

The hardening of heart of Pharaoh, of his courtiers, and of
"the Egyptians" refers to obstinacy. Out of self-interest they
wanted to keep the Israelites as slaves; they did not want to
give them their rightful freedom. Hence they refused to listen
to Moses and Aaron and, ultimately, to God. It implies,
therefore, an obstinate attitude towards one's neighbors and to
God. The many signs and wonders, the many plagues, had no
effect until the last and most terrible one. But immediately
after having granted the Israelites the freedom to leave, they
hardened their hearts again; and so they perished in the waters
of the Sea of Reeds, obstinate till the end.

The terms "obstinate" and "stubborn" heart occur further
in: Dt 2:30; Jos 11:20; 1 S 6:6 (twice); 2 Ch 36:13. In these
texts the terms are applied to various people: to Sihon, king of
Heshbon; to the kings of the North; to the Philistines; and in 2
Ch 36:13 to a king of Israel. The term "hardening of heart" is
used in Dt 15:7, where it refers to the attitude the Israelites
should have towards their poor brothers:

> Is there a poor man among you, one of your brothers, in
> any town of yours in the land that Yahweh your God is
> giving you? Do not harden your heart or close your hand
> against that poor brother of yours. (Dt 15:7).

Here again, "hardening one's heart" refers to a process of closing one's heart out of selfishness.

b. *Wisdom literature*

In the Psalms, it is Israel of the Exodus time that has become "the stubborn generation":

> And not becoming like their ancestors,
> a stubborn and unruly generation,
> a generation with no sincerity of heart,
> in spirit unfaithful to God. (Ps 78:8)

Best known is the text of Psalm 95 used as the invitatory Psalm in the Breviary and quoted in Hebrews 3:8; 3:16; 4:7:

> If only you would listen to him today,
> "Do not harden your heart as at Meribah,
> as you did that day at Massah in the wilderness."
> (Ps 95:7-8)

This text refers to the bitter complaints of the Israelites against Moses in the desert of Rephidim, because of lack of water. It was then that Moses hit the rock and water flowed from it. He called the place "Meribah," which means "contention," and "Massah," meaning "trial." Here Israel "put Yahweh to the test." This text opposes the hardening of the heart to "listening to Yahweh." This shows that when Yahweh will take away our heart of stone, he will give us a "listening heart" instead.

> My people refused to listen to me,
> Israel refused to obey me,
> so I left them to their stubborn selves (lit. "hearts")
> to do whatever they pleased. (Ps 81:11-12)

Here we learn the terrible effect of stubbornness: God leaving those who are stubborn to their hardened selves. Yahweh would have liked to introduce his people into the

Promised Land without delay, but because of their stubborn hearts they had to wander for forty years in the desert; they had to go their own way. Personally they did not reach the Promised Land. Two further texts:

> A stubborn heart will come to a bad end at last. (Si 3:26)

> A stubborn heart is weighed down with troubles. (Si 3:27)

c. The prophets

The prophets experienced deeply how hardened and stubborn Israel's heart was. In the theophany of his mission, Isaiah is told by Yahweh:

> Make the heart of this people gross,
> its ears dull; shut its eyes,
> so that it will not see with its eyes,
> hear with its ears,
> understand with its heart,
> and be converted and healed. (Is 6:10)

What would actually happen is presented here as the "purpose" of Isaiah's mission: a figure of speech. This verse is quoted by Jesus in Mt 13:15. St. John applies it to Jesus' mission in Jn 12:40. St. Paul applies it to his own mission in Ac 28:27. The fact that it occurs in three independent sources of the New Testament shows that its application in the Christian era belongs to very early apostolic tradition. Hardness of heart led Israel to reject the Christian message. Note that especially in John and in Acts we have more than a simple quotation: it is taken as a text that sums up the effect of Jesus' mission and of the mission of St. Paul.

The next quotation from Isaiah is a humble prayer, addressed to Yahweh at the time the enemies were "trampling your sanctuary" (v. 18):

> Why, Yahweh, leave us to stray from your ways
> and harden our hearts against fearing you?

> Return, for the sake of your servants,
> the tribes of your inheritance. (Is 63:17)

Here the author prays that Yahweh may stop hardening our hearts; we could say: "Do not allow us to harden our hearts any longer." The expression "hardness of heart" occurs further in Lamentations 3:65 and in Baruch 2:30:

> And I know very well that this people will not listen;
> it is so stubborn.
> But in the country of their exile they will take all
> this to heart.

Ezekiel has two texts:

> The sons are defiant and obstinate (lit. "hard of heart");
> I am sending you to them . . . (Ezk 2:4)

> But the House of Israel will not listen to you
> because it will not listen to me.
> The whole House of Israel is stubborn and obstinate (lit. "hard of heart"). (Ezk 3:7)

Zechariah concludes our series with this indictment:

> . . . they made their hearts adamant rather than listen to the teaching and the words that Yahweh Sabaoth had sent by his spirit through the prophets in the past. This aroused great anger on the part of Yahweh Sabaoth. (Zc 7:12)

This series of texts about the hardness of Israel's heart is very serious. Of course we have no right to think that Israel was worse than any other people. We should read these texts rather as an instruction about the hardness of our own hearts.

4. The false prophets

A special case are those who present ideas that arose in their own hearts as if they were a revelation from God: a kind of sacrilegious deception. Jeremiah and Ezekiel have several texts about them:

> Yahweh Sabaoth says this:
> Do not listen to what those prophets say:
> they are deluding you,
> they retail visions of their own (lit. "from their own heart")
> and not what comes from the mouth of Yahweh. (Jr 23:16)

See further Jr 14:14; 23:26; and:

> To those who reject the word of Yahweh they say,
> "Peace will be yours,"
> and to those who follow the dictate of a hardened heart,
> "No misfortune will touch you." (Jr 23:17)

> Son of Man, prophesy against the prophets of Israel;
> prophesy and say to those who make up prophecies out of
> their own heads (lit. "hearts"),
> "Hear the word of Yahweh." (Ezk 13:2)

Further: Ezk 13:17.

C. *Sin with regard to one's neighbor*

Of the ten commandments, seven refer to our attitude towards our neighbor. So it is to be expected that also among the texts that speak of the human heart quite a few will refer to sins against one's neighbor. I will divide the relevant texts in three groups: texts from the Pentateuch and the historical books; texts from Wisdom literature; and texts from the prophets.

1. *Texts from the Pentateuch and the historical books*

> You must not bear hatred for your brother in your heart . . .
> You must love your neighbor as yourself. (Lv 19:17)

This commandment belongs to the Law of Holiness, dating from the end of the monarchical period. The terms "brother" and "neighbor" refer to members of one's own people, as the context shows.

> Is there a poor man among you, one of your brothers, in any town of yours in the land that Yahweh your God is giving you? Do not harden your heart or close your hand against that poor brother of yours, but be openhanded with him and lend him enough for his needs. Do not allow this mean thought in your heart, "The seventh year, the year of remission is near," and look coldly on your poor brother and give him nothing; he could appeal against you to Yahweh and it would be a sin for you. When you give to him, you must give with an open heart; for this Yahweh your God will bless you in all you do and in all your giving. Of course there will never cease to be poor in the land; I command you therefore: Always be openhanded with your brother, and with anyone in your country who is in need and poor. (Dt 15:7-11)

This passage requests benevolence, generosity and care for one's poor neighbor. The poor strangers in the country are included as well. The text belongs to a passage about the sabbatical year: after seven years, Hebrew slaves must be given back their freedom, and land must be returned to its previous owner. But this must not become a pretext to refuse help to a brother in need. The text also transcends this case, and recommends generally to give with an open heart and with open hands.

> Nor must he increase the number of his wives, for that could lead his heart astray. Nor must he increase his gold and silver excessively. When he is seated on his royal throne he must write a copy of this Law on a scroll for his own use . . . and he must read it every day of his life. . . . So his heart will not look down on his brothers. (Dt 17:17-20)

These verses belong to a section addressed to the kings of Israel. The commandment against increasing the number of his wives, who might lead his heart astray, is evidently inspired by what happened to Solomon. And his heart must not look down on his brothers: he must not become proud of his status nor despise the people, for they are his brothers.

2. Texts from Wisdom literature

Wisdom literature links the human heart to many kinds of morally evil acts:

— Taking pleasure in evil:
  Taking pleasure in evil earns condemnation (lit. "He who in his heart takes pleasure in evil . . .") (Si 19:5)

— Envy
  Do not let your heart be envious of sinners. (Pr 23:17)

— Deception
  All they do is lie to one another:
  flattering lips, talk from a double heart. (Ps 12:2)

  Deceit in his heart, always scheming evil,
  he sows dissensions. (Pr 6:14)

  Further: Ps 73:7; 55:22; Si 12:16

— Oppression:
  On the contrary, in your hearts you meditate oppression;
  with your hands you dole out tyranny on earth. (Ps 58:2)

— Violence:
  For their hearts are scheming violence. (Pr 24:2)

— Hatred:
  He made his people fertile
  and more vigorous than their oppressors,
  whose hearts he then disposed to hatred of his people
  and doubledealing with his servants. (Ps 105:25)

— Impure desires:
Do not covet her beauty in your heart. (Pr 6:25)

— Adultery:
But the adulterer has no sense (lit. "lacks heart"). (Pr 6:32)
Further: Jb 31:9; Pr 7:10; 7:25.

— Scoffing:
Who scoffs at a neighbor is a fool (lit. "lacks heart").
(Pr 11:12)

— Causing sorrow:
A perverse heart causes sorrow (Si 36:32)

— Reviling others:
Your own heart knows how often you have reviled others.
(Ec 7:22)

3. *The prophets*

The prophets speak out against lack of care and injustice:

— Lack of care:
The upright perish and no one cares
(lit. "and no one takes it to heart"). (Is 57:1)

The whole land has been devastated
and no one takes it to heart. (Jr 12:11)

— Self-interest:
You on the other hand have eyes and heart for nothing but
your own interests, for shedding innocent blood and
perpetrating violence and oppression. (Jr 22:17)

Their hearts are set on dishonest gain. (Ezk 33:31)

— Lies:
Since you distress with lies the heart of the upright man
whom I would never distress. . . . (Ezk 13:22)

— Plotting:

Do not secretly (lit. "in the heart") plot evil against one another. (Zc 8:17)

See further: Dn 11:27; Ho 7:6.

D. Pride and some other wrong attitudes

1. The proud heart

Many texts deal with the proud heart, something very displeasing to God.

First the historical books:

Do not become proud of heart.
Do not then forget Yahweh your God who brought you out of the land of Egypt,
out of the house of slavery. (Dt 8:14)

Further: 2 K 14:10; 2 Ch 25:19; 26:16; 32:25; 32:26; 1 M 5:21.

Wisdom literature:

Haughty looks, proud heart,
I cannot tolerate these. (Ps 101:5)

The arrogant heart is abhorrent to Yahweh,
be sure it will not go unpunished. (Pr 16:5)

The human heart is haughty until destruction comes,
humility goes before honor. (Pr 18:12)

Further: Ps 131:1; Pr 21:4; Si 11:30

The prophets express the idea of pride with various images:

— A haughty heart: (Jr 48:29)
— A boastful heart: (Is 10:12)
— Arrogance of heart: (Is 9:8; Dn 8:25)
— Swollen with pride: (Ezk 28:2; 28:17; Dn 5:20)

Obadiah 3 speaks to Edom:

> Your pride of heart has led you astray,
> You whose home is in the holes in the rocks,
> who make the heights your dwelling;
> who say in your heart,
> "Who will bring me down to the ground?"

An image, worked out into a parable of considerable length, is found in Ezekiel 31:1-9: the parable of the cedar tree. The words that follow the parable speak of the heart of the cedar, image of Pharaoh's heart:

> Very well then, the Lord Yahweh says this:
> "Since it has raised itself to its full height, has lifted its top to the clouds, and (lit. "in the heart") has grown arrogant in its height, I have handed it over to the prince of the nations, to do with it as its wickedness deserves."
>
> (Ezk 31:10)

We could call this "the parable of the proud cedar." Because of its pride it had to be cut down.

2. Some other wrong attitudes

A bit more vigor, please:

> Woe to faint hearts and listless hands. (Si 2:12)
>
> Woe to the listless heart that has no faith,
> for such will have no protection. (Si 2:13)

Think first!

> He who trusts his own promptings (lit. "his own heart")
> is a fool.
> He whose ways are wise will be safe. (Pr 28:26)

Lament about my youth:

> Alas, I hated discipline,
> my heart spurned all correction. (Pr 5:12)

Attachment to money:

> Turn my heart to your decrees
> and away from getting money. (Ps 119:36)

> . . . for gold has destroyed many,
> and has swayed the hearts of kings. (Si 8:2)

ART. 2

THE PROMISE OF A NEW HEART: THE HEART OF FLESH

1. Jeremiah

The great prophet who first revealed God's promise to give us a different heart is Jeremiah. He was well prepared for this prophetic task. His personal suffering had purified his soul. His experience of the sinfulness of his people and of the dramatic events that took place during his lifetime, together with his ardent faith in God, made him an exquisite instrument in God's hand. A man of sorrows, but also of hope and vision. The New Jerusalem Bible says of him:

> Before expressing it in his prophecy of the new covenant, 31:31-34, Jeremiah practiced a really inward and heart-felt religion; this is what makes him near and dear to Christians. . . . His warm religion makes Jeremiah not unlike Hosea, who influenced him; his conception of the Law as an "inward" force, his respect for the function of love in true religion, his concern for the person as an individual, show affinities with Deuteronomy. . . . His doctrine of a new covenant written in the heart made him the father of all that was best in Judaism. His influence may be seen in Ezekiel, in Deutero-Isaiah and in several of the Psalms. (NJB p. 1171)

Jeremiah is the prophet with a fire burning in his heart (20:9); the prophet with a broken heart (23:9). He has the highest number of texts about the heart of God, eight in all. He has the fiercest texts about the wicked heart of his people. And he is the prophet of the promise of a different heart. By way of introduction I quote two texts in which Jeremiah exhorts his people to purify their hearts.

> Wash your heart clean of wickedness, Jerusalem, and so be saved. How long will you harbor in your breast your pernicious thoughts? (Jr 4:14)

> Circumcise yourselves for Yahweh, off with the foreskin of your hearts (men of Judah and inhabitants of Jerusalem), lest my wrath should leap out like a fire. . . . (Jr 4:4)

We have here two images: the image of washing the heart clean, and the image of circumcising the heart. In Jr 9:25 the prophet spoke of the Israelites as "uncircumcised at heart." Here he tells them to circumcise their hearts, to be a true covenant people, to wash their hearts clean of wickedness by changing their way of thinking, their selfish outlook on life, their obstinate attitude to God.

The first time Jeremiah announces that Yahweh will give his people a different heart is in chapter 24, the chapter about the vision of the good and the bad figs. The bad figs are the nobility that was left behind in Jerusalem. Those already exiled in Babylon are to become the good figs:

> Yahweh, the God of Israel, says this:
> As these figs are good, so I mean to concern myself with the welfare of the exiles of Judah whom I have sent from this place to the land of the Chaldeans. My eyes will watch over them for their good, to bring them back to this land, to build them up and not to break them down. . . . I will give them a heart to acknowledge that I am Yahweh. They shall be my people and I will be their God, for they will return to me with all their heart. (Jr 24:5-7)

The change of heart (Jeremiah does not use the expression "new heart," used later by Ezekiel) will start with the Jews in exile. In fact several books in the Old Testament, like

Daniel and Esther, have moving texts about the conversion these exiles went through. A reference to a deepening of the covenant is implied in the sentence: "They shall be my people and I will be their God." The change of heart is presented as a gift of God. It implies a new acknowledgment of Yahweh, and a return to him "with all their heart."

The most important texts are found in the book of consolation (chapter 30-33), where Jeremiah addresses both the Northern kingdom and Judah.

> See, the days are coming — it is Yahweh who speaks — when I will make a new covenant with the House of Israel (and the House of Judah), but not a covenant like the one I made with their ancestors on the day I took them by the hand to bring them out of the land of Egypt. They broke that covenant of mine, so I had to show them who was master. It is Yahweh who speaks. No, this is the covenant I will make with the House of Israel when those days arrive — it is Yahweh who speaks. Deep within them I will plant my Law, writing it on their hearts. Then I will be their God and they shall be my people. There will be no further need for neighbor to try to teach neighbor, or brother to say to brother, "Learn to know Yahweh!" No, they will all know me, the least no less than the greatest — it is Yahweh who speaks — since I will forgive their iniquity and never call their sin to mind. (Jr 31:31-34)

The disaster of the exile has struck. The people are suffering, the covenant has been broken, the City and the Temple are destroyed. In this situation Jeremiah becomes a consoler, and opens a perspective of hope. He brings a vision of a new future that will come as a grace of God: a new covenant. Their sins will be forgiven and forgotten; the Law will be written on their hearts. They shall truly be God's people, and everybody will "know" Yahweh.

This vision, this promise, is forever part of Israel's hope. It had a deep influence at the time of the exile. But because of the reference to the new covenant, it is part of the faith and hope of the new Israel as well. It is also our hope. We believe that its realization came, partially in Babylonian exile, yes, but fully with the Mediator of the new covenant. Hebrews 8:8-12 applies this passage to the new covenant, brought by Christ.

> I mean to gather them from all the countries where I have driven them in my anger, my fury and great wrath. I will bring them back to this place and make them live in safety. Then they shall be my people, and I will be their God. I will give them a different heart and different behavior so that they will always fear me, for the good of themselves and their children after them. I will make an everlasting covenant with them; I will not cease my efforts for their good, and I will put respect for me into their hearts, so that they turn from me no more. It will be my pleasure to bring about their good, and I will plant them firmly in this land, with all my heart and soul. (Jr 32:37-41)

This passage and the previous one are the peak of Jeremiah's spirituality. The Mosaic covenant has been violated; people are in exile. Now Yahweh will make a new beginning. The dispersed will be gathered, a new and eternal covenant will be made, as after the Flood, and Yahweh will give his people a "different heart" and "different behavior." The New Jerusalem Bible translates: "I shall give them singleness of heart and singleness of conduct." Quite a few exegetes prefer this last translation: Yahweh will give his people one single heart and one behavior. This can make us think of Acts 4:32: "The whole group of believers was united, heart and soul." They were "one heart and one soul." The expression "one heart" is used also in 2 Chronicles 30:12: "to inspire them with a united will" (lit. "to give them one heart"). This refers to unity, consensus, "concordia."

The new covenant will be characterized by forgiveness, greater respect for Yahweh, a deeper knowledge of Yahweh, faithfulness, internal and external unity, the constant care and generosity of God who will bring his people back to their own land, and interiorization of religion. The new Law will not be an external code, but an inspiration working on the human heart (Jr 31:33). The eternal covenant is mentioned also in Isaiah 55:3: "With you I will make an everlasting covenant." All this will be granted by Yahweh as his gift to his people.

The book of Baruch was written much later than Jeremiah, maybe as late as the first century B.C., but it was inspired by Jeremiah (that is why it is presented as written by Jeremiah's disciple Baruch). Two texts that reflect this influence are relevant here.

> But in the country of their exile they will take all this to heart, and acknowledge that I am the Lord their God. I will give them a heart and an attentive ear. . . .
>
> (Ba 2:30-31)
>
> You are indeed the Lord our God and we long to praise you, Lord, since you have put respect for you in our hearts to encourage us to call on your name. We long to praise you in our exile, for we have emptied our hearts of the evil inclinations of our ancestors who sinned against you. (Ba 3:7)

This second text presents the renewal of heart as having already started. The exile was really a time of conversion, a return to the heart.

2. Ezekiel

Ezekiel was a priest who shared the dramatic experience of the Babylonian exile. He gives us his vision of "the new Temple," with the mysterious stream of living water flowing from it, something not unrelated to our topic. But I will limit myself here to the texts about the heart. And in this area he continues the line of Jeremiah and even deepens it. As Jeremiah has some texts exhorting the Jews to cleanse their hearts and to circumcise their hearts, so Ezekiel has a text commanding the Jews to renew their hearts:

> Shake off all the sins you have committed against me, and
> make yourselves a new heart and a new spirit . . . repent,
> and live! (Ezk 18:31)

Here, for the first time, we meet the expression "a new heart and a new spirit." But here the people are told to achieve that themselves, even though it is something we cannot attain by our own efforts alone. In the two classical statements of Ezekiel, to which we will now turn, God promises the new heart and the new spirit as a gift. Evidently here also we can speak of "gift and task." Conversion is something we must achieve, by the grace of God.

> The Lord Yahweh says this:
>
> "I will gather you together from the peoples, I will bring
> you all back from the countries where you have been
> scattered and I will give you the land of Israel. They will
> come and will purge it of all the horrors and the filthy
> practices. I will give them a single heart and I will put a
> new spirit in them; I will remove the heart of stone from
> their bodies and give them a heart of flesh instead, so that
> they will keep my laws and respect my observances and
> put them into practice. Then they shall be my people and
> I will be their God." (Ezk 11:17-20)

This text is very close to Jr 32:37-41. Here again we meet the promise of the gathering of the exiles and of the "single heart." The new covenant is not mentioned, though the covenant formula, "they will be my people and I will be their God" is there. The "one single heart" expresses unity, "concordia," consensus. New is the promise of the new spirit, and the phrase "I will remove the heart of stone from their bodies and give them a heart of flesh instead. . . ." The heart of stone is the hardened, obstinate heart. The new heart is a heart of flesh: a truly human heart, pliable to the will of God, faithful to God's Law, open to God and to one's neighbor. One single heart implies mutual acceptance.

> Then I am going to take you from among the nations and
> gather you together from all the foreign countries, and
> bring you home to your own land. I shall cleanse you of all
> your defilement and all your idols. I shall give you a new
> heart, and put a new spirit in you; I shall remove the heart
> of stone from your bodies and give you a heart of flesh
> instead. I shall put my spirit in you, and make you keep
> my laws and sincerely respect my observances. You will
> live in the land which I gave your ancestors. You shall be
> my people and I will be your God. (Ezk 36:24-27)

This is the most complete expression of the promise of the
new heart. Most of the elements of the previous quotations are
here: the gathering together of the exiles, the return to their
own land, the cleansing, the new heart and the new spirit, the
faithfulness to God's Law. The expression "new covenant" is
not there, but again the covenant formula, "You shall be my
people . . ." is there.

New in this passage, in comparison with the texts of
Jeremiah are: the image of clean water (though Jr 4:14 does
say: "Wash your heart clean . . ."); the promise of the "new
heart" and the "new spirit" ("my own spirit"); and the sentence
(already mentioned in Ezk 11:19), "I shall remove the heart of
stone from your bodies and give you a heart of flesh instead."
The promise that Yahweh will write his Law on our heart (Jr
31:33) is replaced by the text about the new spirit, God's own
spirit.

A new heart and a new spirit: Scripture often puts the
terms "heart" and "soul" together: "leb" and "nepesh." Often
these two terms have almost the same meaning. Generally
speaking, the "soul" refers to man from the standpoint of his
vegetative life and his exterior, says Kittel. An "animated"
man can move and live. The "heart" refers to the inner worth of
a person, to his consciousness. But in this text of Ezekiel it is
not the word "soul" ("nepesh") that is used, but the word
"spirit" ("ruah"). Kittel characterizes the difference between
"soul" and "spirit" thus: "Without nepesh an individual dies,
but without ruah a nepesh is no longer an authentic nepesh"

(Kittel, *Grande Lessico del Nuovo Testamento*, s.v. "psyche," p. 626). The heart expresses inwardness, the spirit expresses "motivating power." A new heart and a new spirit, therefore, refer to a complete interior renewal: a new heart with a new motivation and inspiration.

The original meaning of "ruah" is "breath." When Adam was created, God breathed life into him (Gn 2:7). But now God promises to give us a new breath, hence: to breathe into us a new life. He will even give us "his own spirit." This, in the light of the New Testament, makes us think of the Holy Spirit. Thus we have the background necessary to understand Jesus' promise of living water, of sending the Spirit, of Pentecost. The new creation starts in the heart. Thus renewed, we will know God as "Abba," and we will pray: "Thy Kingdom come, Thy will be done."

3. *Some related texts from the other prophets*

a. *Hosea*

Long before Jeremiah and Ezekiel, Hosea had already spoken of Yahweh's plan to renew Israel interiorly. The New Jerusalem Bible says about Hosea:

> The Book of Hosea has had a profound influence on the Old Testament; there are echoes of Hosea in the exhortations of later prophets to a religion of the heart, with God's love as its motive force. Jeremiah was deeply influenced by Hosea. It is not surprising that the New Testament quotes Hosea or, not infrequently, draws upon him. The wedding imagery of God's love for his people is taken up by Jeremiah, Ezekiel and the second part of Isaiah. The New Testament and the early Christian community apply it to the union between Christ and his Church. Christian mysticism has extended the application to the individual soul. (p. 1181)

The main texts from Hosea are found in the second chapter. It seems that some parts of this chapter are of later origin.

> That is why I am going to lure her
> and lead her out into the wilderness (a new Exodus!)
> and speak to her heart. (Ho 2:16)
>
> I will betroth you to myself for ever. . . . (Ho 2:21-22)

We find here the idea of a new attempt of Yahweh's love; there is a reference to Israel's heart, and a hint at an eternal covenant. "You shall be my people and I shall be your God" is worked out here in terms of a spousal relationship.

b. Deutero-Isaiah

The second part of the book of Isaiah too has magnificent texts about a new future that God will create (Is 48:6-7); the return to the land (chapter 49); the coming of salvation (52:7-10); the role of the servant; the renewal of the bonds of love (54:4-10); the eternal covenant (55:3-5). In this context:

> Stir your memories again, you sinner
> (lit. "Return to the heart, you sinner"). (Is 46:8)

The great renewal implies a return to the heart. Remembering things long past (as the context says: remembering God's great deeds of the past), Israel must also remember her first love. She must come to her senses (1 K 8:47). This, too, is implied in the phrase "return to the heart."

We could add to this picture certain beautiful texts from Third Isaiah, for example chapter 62 on the glorious resurrection of Jerusalem, and the eschatological discourse of chapter 66:18-24 about the new heavens and the new earth. These texts have been influenced by Jeremiah.

c. *Joel*

The prophet Joel most probably belongs to the post-exilic period. He is the great prophet of Pentecost, and of the return to Yahweh:

> But now, now — it is Yahweh who speaks —
> come back to me with all your heart,
> fasting, weeping, mourning.
> Let your hearts be broken, not your garments torn,
> turn to Yahweh your God again,
> for he is all tenderness and compassion,
> slow to anger, rich in graciousness,
> and ready to relent. (Jl 2:12-13)
>
> After this I will pour out my spirit on all mankind.
> Your sons and daughters shall prophesy,
> your old men shall dream dreams,
> and your young men see visions.
> Even on the slaves, men and women,
> will I pour out my spirit in those days. (Jl 3:1-2)

The promise of Yahweh's own spirit is extended here to all mankind.

d. *Daniel*

The book of Daniel seems to belong to the time of Antiochus Epiphanes, second century B.C. What it says about the suffering of the exiles in Babylon is applicable to the time of the persecution under Antiochus. The conversion is described as already an actual reality in Babylon; the renewal of heart has started.

> But may the contrite soul, the humbled spirit be as acceptable to you as holocausts of rams and bullocks, as thousands of fattened lambs: such let our sacrifice be to you today, and may it be your will that we will follow you wholeheartedly, since those who put their trust in you will

not be disappointed. And now we put our whole heart into
following you, into fearing you and seeking your face
once more. (Dn 3:39-41)

This text is very close to Psalm 51:19. Not only the Law is
interiorized in the new heart, but also worship: priesthood and
sacrifice. The new sacrifice is the sacrifice of the broken heart,
and all believers can offer this sacrifice to God. The absence of
fattened lambs, in other words, poverty, helped the Jews to
discover what they really should be offering to God, namely
their hearts. This is worship in spirit and in truth, the kind of
worship Jesus wanted.

4. *Deuteronomy*

The book of Deuteronomy shows much affinity with the
spirituality of Jeremiah. This is especially true of the texts that
speak of the human heart.

Circumcise your heart then and be obstinate no longer.
(Dt 10:16)

Compare Jr 4:4: "Circumcise yourselves for Yahweh; off
with the foreskin of your hearts. . . ."

Yahweh your God will circumcise your heart and the
heart of all your descendants, until you love Yahweh your
God with all your heart and soul, and so have life.
(Dt 30:6).

The circumcision of the heart is not the only theme
common to Deuteronomy and Jeremiah; there are several other
themes as well. In the first place, the return to Yahweh "with
all their heart." See Jr 24:7: "They will return to me with all
their heart."
Compare also:

> . . . if you return to Yahweh your God with all your heart
> and soul. (Dt 30:10)

> . . . if you return to Yahweh your God, if you obey his
> voice with all your heart and soul in everything I enjoin on
> you today. . . . (Dt 30:2)

Then there is the theme of the interiorization of the Law.
Jeremiah said: "Deep within them I will plant my Law, writing
it in their hearts" (Jr 31:33).
Compare:

> Let these words I urge on you today be written on your heart.
> (Dt 6:6)
> No, the Word is very near to you, it is in your mouth and in
> your heart for your observance. (Dt 30:14)

Jeremiah made these statements in passages where he
speaks of the new covenant. It looks as if Deuteronomy presents the Mosaic covenant in line with Jeremiah's vision of the
new covenant! And as Hosea interprets the covenant in terms
of bonds of love, so does Deuteronomy. Many times the great
first commandment is underlined:

> You shall love Yahweh your God with all your heart,
> with all your soul, with all your strength. (Dt 6:5)

> Further: Dt 10:12; 4:29

The time of the Exile was the beginning of the realization
of the new heart: the suffering servant of Yahweh is a
foreshadowing of Christ. At that time, Israel's heart was broken, its heart of stone was taken away, and Yahweh did not
scorn their "crushed and broken heart" (Ps 51:17; Dn 3:39).
But in view of the legalism that later prevailed in Judaism, this
revival was not yet the full realization of God's promise expressed in Jeremiah and Ezekiel. The new covenant was inau-
gurated by the One whose Heart was pierced on the cross.
Through his Spirit the Law is truly written on our hearts.

5. *The historical books*

The books of Joshua, Samuel and Kings show affinity with Deuteronomy: they are "deuteronomic writings." Again, the heart-texts confirm this.

> Then cast away the alien gods among you and give your hearts to Yahweh, the God of Israel. (Jos 24:23)

The covenant at Shechem is expressed in terms of giving the heart to Yahweh, an expression characteristic of the interiorized religion of the Deuteronomist. Compare Jos 22:5.

> If you are returning to Yahweh with all your heart, put aside the foreign gods you now have and the Astartes too, and set your heart on Yahweh, and serve him alone. (1 S 7:3)

In this text it is as if we hear Jeremiah speak about the divided heart of the Israelites: "with all your heart" is the opposite of a divided heart. See further 1 S 12:24.

1 Kings has some beautiful texts about conversion, about returning to Yahweh with all one's heart, texts inspired by the deep spirituality of the Exile time, especially in chapter 8: Solomon's prayer at the inauguration of the Temple in Jerusalem.

> . . . if in the land of their exile they come to themselves (lit. "they turn to their hearts") and repent . . . and if they turn again to you with all their heart and soul in the country of the enemies who have deported them. . . . (1 K 8:47-48)

The coordination of the two phrases, "if they turn to their hearts" and "if they turn again to you," is interesting. "Turning to the heart" and "turning to God" belong to the same process, the process of conversion. In Scripture, Joshua, Samuel and Solomon speak the language of the Deuteronomist, who shares the spirituality of Jeremiah. It is truly remarkable that Israel, at the moment of deepest humiliation and of political defeat, reached the highest point of its spirituality: the spirituality of the broken heart, the spiritual sacrifice.

This text about the return to the heart fits beautifully into that spirituality. "If in the land of their exile they turn to their hearts. . . ." The Jerusalem Bible translates this: "If . . . they come to themselves . . ." By turning to one's heart, one may find one's authentic self, for the heart is also our conscience. The New Jerusalem Bible translates: "If . . . they come to their senses . . ." In Is 46:8 the phrase "return to the heart" is translated in the Jerusalem Bible by "Stir your memories again," in line with the context. All these translations are possible. They all express partially what is included in the return to the heart. This beautiful expression is quoted in 2 Ch 6:37-38. The return to the heart and the return to Yahweh are coordinated again.

The return to the heart is an important concept in the spirituality of the heart. It is an invitation to recollection, to conversion; to do away with superficial slogans, with misguided excuses, with blind activism; to listen again to the heart, the seat of wisdom; to listen again to God, for God speaks to the heart, as we learned from Hosea. The return to God starts with a return to the heart. When we listen to the heart, we may find the way and the truth: what is really expected from me? That is the way to find our authentic selves. And having returned to the heart, we may be able to speak from the heart, to help someone else to listen to his heart.

Some further texts:

May your hearts be wholly with Yahweh your God,
following his laws and keeping his commandments as at this present day. (1 K 8:61)

This turning to Yahweh is a grace of God:

May he turn our hearts towards him so that we may follow all his ways and keep the commandments. . . . (1 K 8:58)

And the prophet Elijah:

Answer me, Yahweh, answer me, so that this people may
know that you, Yahweh, are God and are winning back
their hearts. (1 K 18:37)

The Deuteronomist lived in Jeremiah's time and shared
his spiritual outlook. Under the influence of these two, we hear
God's plan of turning our hearts to him, of renewing our heart,
of giving us a heart of flesh, from the lips of Moses, of Joshua,
of Solomon, of Elijah. The Deuteronomist explicates the great
commandment of loving Yahweh with all our heart, and of
turning to our heart. He does not speak of a new covenant, but
interprets the Mosaic covenant in the new spirit. For the new
covenant we have to wait for the new Adam, who will put the
love of neighbor more clearly into focus. The new Adam
certainly did not live in a paradise, but he did interpret "the
new heaven and the new earth" in terms of the Kingdom of his
Father. His new Spirit will renew the face of the earth.

CHAPTER FOUR

JESUS' HEART IN THE NEW TESTAMENT

Every human heart is a mystery. But Jesus' Heart is mysterious in a unique way, for we believe that his Heart has divine depth. Let us approach this mystery with respect. Here we have the core of the Son of God; the source of living water. "If any man is thirsty, let him come." What moved Jesus most deeply? What were his basic attitudes, his hopes, his desires?

St. Margaret Mary often spoke of the *divine* Heart of Jesus. When Vatican II mentioned Jesus' Heart, it spoke of his *human* Heart: "He loved with a human heart" (GS art. 22). This is not a difference of faith, but a difference of spiritual climate and of emphasis. There is no question of going against the Council of Chalcedon, where the two natures of Christ were defined as being united in one Person. In our days we like to start from the historical Jesus; after all it is Jesus in his humanity who is the revelation of God. We look at the historical Jesus in faith, and we discover the mystery of this person. And we believe that Jesus was so fully human, that even his knowledge, his love and his feelings developed historically. For the historical dimension is integral to a "human nature" (compare Lk 2:40, 52).

In the history of spirituality we can see in the first millennium great stress on Jesus' wounded side, from which blood and water flowed. The Fathers discovered the paschal mystery in the Heart of our Savior. The French School, on the other hand, loved to contemplate the "attitudes" of Jesus. We have here two different approaches to the mystery of Jesus' Heart.

How do we start our study? I think we should study Jesus' life first: his deepest thoughts (we mean "heart" in the biblical sense), his deepest feelings. Then we will consider his redemptive death: the pierced side; Jesus dispensing the Spirit. Thus we hope to integrate the "objective" and the "subjective" approach.

ART. 1   THE REVELATION OF JESUS' HEART DURING HIS LIFE ON EARTH

1. The Heart of a Son[1]

It would not be difficult to present a long list of texts from the four gospels and from St. Paul, where Jesus is presented as the Son, even, at times, as "the Son of God." This title clearly belonged to the faith of the apostolic Church. "God sent his Son," says St. Paul in Gal 4:4-5, ". . . to enable us to be adopted as sons." For St. John, this was the main point of his gospel, for he wrote it in order that we might believe "that Jesus is the Christ, the Son of God" (Jn 20:31). Later theology considered this title solely in terms of the problem of the "two natures" of Jesus; "Son of God" was said to designate Jesus' divine nature.

Though all this is true, it does not explain that Jesus had "the Heart of a Son." What I want to express with "the Heart of a Son" is, that Jesus *knew* himself to be the Son, felt very much like a Son, looked on God as "Abba," his dear Father, lived in a Son-Father relationship. The divine relationship Son-Father filled his human heart; it was his secret, his joy; a constant awareness; a basic attitude that determined his behavior. To prove that, we have to look for texts about the historical Jesus in which he opens his Heart.

In the first place we point to the fact that Jesus called God "Abba"; Jesus' "Abba-experience." In his book *The Prayers of Jesus* (SCM 1974), J. Jeremias has studied this topic in depth. In the gospels the word "Father," for God, is used 170 times by

Jesus himself; in all his prayers he addressed God in this way.
Jesus spoke to God as a child to his father. This fact alone
reveals already his relationship to God: a relationship of sonship, of familiarity and intimacy, of simplicity and confidence,
of surrender and obedience.

It is important to note that Jesus commended the use of
"Abba" also to his disciples, as shown by Luke's version of the
Lord's prayer (Lk 11:2) and as confirmed by St. Paul in Gal 4:6
and Rm 8:15. But he emphasized the uniqueness of his own
Sonship as well. Jesus never includes himself in *our* relation-
ship to the Father, but always distinguishes between "My
Father" and "your Father," which reveals a distinction of
relationships.

There are several texts which bring out the uniqueness of
Jesus' Sonship very impressively, for example Mk 13:32; also
Jn 5:18: "He spoke of God as his own Father, and so made
himself God's equal." Most impressive is the Q logion of Mt
11:25-27/Lk 10:21-22, the "mutual knowledge logion": "No
one knows the Son except the Father, just as no one knows the
Father except the Son and those to whom the Son chooses to
reveal him." These verses express a uniquely close relationship between the Father and the Son, and a unique position of
the Son whom nobody knows but the Father. Unrestricted
authority has been given to him.

For Jesus personally his Sonship was an existential con-
viction and a unique relationship. Out of this experience the
dogma of a Sonship of essence ("begotten from the Father
before all ages") has developed, and the process clearly began
in the New Testament itself, especially in John. Many riches
are hidden in this "Abba-experience." Jesus often stressed the
goodness of God, and his willingness to forgive us and grant us
a hearing. In all these respects God surpasses any human
father: (Mt 7:11; Lk 11:13; 11:5-8; 18:2-8). We may safely
burden God with all our cares, for he knows all our needs (Lk
12:22-31/Mt 6:25-33). Since not a single sparrow falls to the
ground without God's permission, he will certainly protect *us*
(Mt 10:29-31/Lk 12:6f). Especially the mercy of his Father

must have struck Jesus, and so he defended his association with publicans and sinners (Mk 2:17). The mercy of God is proclaimed in the parable of the workers in the vineyard, of the Pharisee and the Publican, but most convincingly in the parable of the Prodigal Son, which is also the parable of the Merciful Father (Lk 15:11-32).

From this experience of Jesus' Heart, a new way of relating to God has arisen. Our knowledge of God has been transformed. From his fullness we have received, and we are reborn. We opened this section on Jesus' Sonship with a quotation from Gal 4:4-5. We should now see how this text continues: "The proof that you are sons is that God has sent the Spirit of his Son into our hearts; the Spirit that cries 'Abba, Father.' " Jesus' Heart was the home of the Spirit, who moved him to live as Son. [2] It was that Spirit he bestowed on us.

Here we note the deepest dimension of the transformation of our knowledge of God: Jesus experienced God as his own Father, and, consequently, he felt himself Son; and he experienced the Spirit as powerfully moving him. On the human level, the mystery of the Trinity was lived first in the Heart of Christ, which, therefore, is truly the source of the new life.

2. The Obedience of the Son

Jesus' Sonship was expressed very clearly in his obedient attitude toward the Father. This obedience did not just consist in acts of obedience, but was truly a basic attitude, a dimension of his Heart, a surrender of himself.

In this context, many spiritual authors like to quote Ps 40:6-8:

> You who wanted no sacrifice or oblation,
>   opened my ear.
> You asked no holocaust or sacrifice for sin;
>   then I said, 'Here I am! I am coming!'
> In the scroll of the book am I not commanded

to obey your will?
My God, this I desire,
    I carry your law in the midst of my heart
    (Hebrew: "me'ay," "entrails").

This text is quoted in Heb 10:5-7, and commented upon. Jesus, the new Adam, carried God's law in the midst of his heart, to be cherished, to be meditated upon, to be lived. St. Paul says in Rm 5:19: "For just as by the disobedience of the one the many were constituted sinners, so also by the obedience of the one, the many will be constituted just." Jesus' obedience is the source of redemption. It is related to the new form of sacrifice, the "spiritual sacrifice," which consists in offering oneself in obedience to God. It is related to the new form of priesthood, which consists in giving oneself. Ph 2:7-8 says that Jesus assumed the condition of a servant, obedient to the point of accepting death, death on a cross.

Jesus was a servant with an open ear, always ready to listen, always doing what was pleasing to the Father (Jn 8:29). Doing the will of the Father was his mission, his passion; he was hungry for it, for it was his food: "My food is to do the will of the one who sent me, and to complete his work" (Jn 4:34). The will of his Father was manifested to him through a series of intermediaries: persons ("and he lived under their authority" Lk 2:51), events, institutions, writings of his people, human authorities. When the crunch came, he was able to say: "let your will be done, not mine" (Lk 22:42). It was not always easy. Even Jesus had to learn to obey through suffering. "Although he was Son, he learnt to obey through suffering; but having been made perfect, he became for all who obey him the source of eternal salvation and was acclaimed by God with the title of high priest" (Heb 5:8-10).

The obedience of a servant, the obedience of one sent, priestly obedience, but primarily: the obedience of a Son. He knew the Father as no one else; he knew the will of the Father as no one else. He speaks the words of the Father; he performs the works of the Father; he lived, always turned to the Father:

"pros ton Theon" (Jn 1:1, 18, as explained by I. de la Potterie, cf. n. 1, p. 125). His adherence to the Father's will was adherence in love; a manifestation of his divine Sonship. "The Father and I are one" (Jn 10:30).

3. The Kingdom of the Father

Jesus' preaching was summarized in Mk 1:15 as follows: "The time is accomplished and the Kingdom of God is at hand. Be converted, and believe the Good News." The "fullness of time" (Gal 4:4) has come; from that time on "the Kingdom of God is preached" (Lk 16:16; Mt 4:12). The decisive time has come; we must hurry, so as not to miss it.

Jesus preached "the glad tidings of the Kingdom" (Lk 4:18). He was obsessed by the idea of the Kingdom of God. That seems to sum up all the changes he had in mind. The Kingdom is the dream of God; it becomes a reality in Jesus of Nazareth. The idea that we are all invited to it, is most beautifully expressed in the parable of the Banquet (Mt 22:1-13).

The meaning of the Kingdom is explained in the parables, in Jesus' "works," and in his moral message.

The parables explain that the Kingdom is like a seed (see Mt 13); it is like a mustard seed. It is like leaven, for it transforms society. It is like a hidden treasure, like a pearl, so beautiful; like a dragnet thrown into the sea.

The "works" of Jesus show that the Kingdom has come. Exorcisms show that the prince of this world has to give way to Jesus; he sets us free from evil powers. Satan's reign has to give way to God's reign (Jn 12:31). "If I by the Spirit of God cast out devils, then the Kingdom of God is here" (Mt 12:28/Lk 11:20). The new heaven and the new earth announce themselves in Jesus' miracles: the blind see, the deaf hear, the lame walk, the lepers are cleansed, the hungry are fed. Jesus forgives sins, eats with the outcast, talks with authority, is master of the Sabbath.

To enter the Kingdom, a deep change of heart is required, the "metanoia." This change consists in a new attitude to God as Abba; a new attitude to our fellowmen as our brothers; a new attitude towards the things of this world (Lk 18:29). The Beatitudes sum it all up. All values are reversed: blessed are, not the successful, the rich, but the poor, the hungry, the persecuted. The first will be last.

That the Kingdom is the basic concern of Jesus' Heart becomes even more clear when we realize the identification of the Kingdom with Jesus himself. De la Potterie works this out in his excellent article,[3] where he supports this view with quotations from the Fathers and from contemporary Scripture scholars. The Kingdom consists in establishing the sovereignty of God in a new and powerful manner; but the amazing thing is that Jesus is the one to exercise it. Mark refers to Jesus' authority (Mk 1:22, 27). He mentions that people experienced this in Jesus' way of teaching. It appears even more clearly in his works (Mk 1:17; 2:7, 10, 14, 28). This explains also why Jesus can answer the question of the Pharisees, when the Kingdom of God was to come, with the words: ". . . you must know, the Kingdom of God is among you" (Lk 17:20-21). According to de la Potterie, scholars nowadays agree that we should not translate "within you," but "among you." The Kingdom of God makes its presence felt already in Jesus' ministry.

If this is the case, when Jesus acted as the plenipotentiary of God, when he made the truth, the love, the mercy of God present in such an amazing way, then Jesus is not merely an agent of the Kingdom, but the deep realization of it. His Heart was new; by a deep metanoia we can enter into this mystery. No wonder that the Apostles after the paschal experience preached that Jesus is Lord, and started talking about the "Kingdom of Christ." For Jesus had acted as Lord. If it is true that Jesus preached the Kingdom and the Apostles preached Jesus, then this is not a substantial change.

The central notion of St. John's gospel is "life." It is sometimes said that in John, the notion of life has taken the place of the notion of the Kingdom, which is central in the synoptic gospels. Well, here too Jesus can say: "I am the life." To enter into it, we must be reborn. Rebirth takes here the place of the metanoia of the synoptics, and deepens it. Thus St. John supports in his own way that Jesus is the Kingdom.

We must be deeply renewed, in the Spirit of Jesus. We must share Jesus' vision of the Kingdom: God's truth, God's love and mercy must reign supreme. This is the vision of a reborn universe, a new world to be born (Rm 8:19-23); a new heaven and a new earth (Rv 21:1). For the metanoia, the change of mind and heart, the new way of thinking, the new way of relating, will change everything. Society will change; the way of exercising authority will change; the goods of the earth will be shared, as in the first Christian community at Jerusalem. Everything must be as God wants it to be.

The Church is sent as the sacrament of the Kingdom. Sacrament, says Vatican II (LG, art. 1) means: sign and instrument. Sign: the new life must already be present in the Church, for all to see. Instrument: as servant of the Kingdom, the Church is sent to continue Jesus' mission of truth and service, to make all things new. To drive out evil, to forgive, to heal, to unite, to bring peace. This is what Jesus' mission was about; this is what filled his Heart; this was his passion, in God's name. "Thy Kingdom come!"

4. Dimensions of Jesus' love

In recent centuries it was generally said that the human heart is the symbol of love. This seems to me a superficial use of the word "heart"; in this study I try to take "heart," not as a symbol, but in the biblical sense of the core of a person. In that sense, a heart can be a heart of stone; it can be filled with egoism, with jealousy, or with feelings of revenge. Since the human heart is a mystery, we must not define it a priori as "love"; whether it is loving in fact, remains to be seen!

In this section I would like to study the fact that Jesus' Heart was filled with an unprecedented love, and I would like to point out some dimensions of this mystery. We need not be afraid that the traditional values of the "devotion to the Sacred Heart" will be lost in the biblical approach. To the contrary, its authentic values will be discovered in a new way, in the way Jesus actually revealed himself when he lived among us. As love was his commandment, so it was his way of life, his praxis, his attitude. As love is the soul of perfection, so it was the force that moved him.

Jesus' love was transcendent in every way: by its intimacy, its universality, its definitive character, its fertility, etc. Since we have treated the "Abba experience" already in the section on Jesus' Sonship, I will not treat again the aspect of Jesus' filial love for the Father, even though we have here the source of the universality of our love of neighbor.

The bibliography about love, both in the Old and in the New Testament, is immense. The encyclical of Pope Pius XII, *Haurietis Aquas*, presented Jesus' Heart as symbol of his threefold love: divine, human-spiritual, and human-emotional. Consequently, in the commentaries on this encyclical, especially in *Cor Jesu* I, much is to be found on Jesus' love. Personally, I made use especially of the beautiful article of Fr. Pedro Arrupe, S.J., "The Heart of Christ, Center of the Christian Mystery and Key to the Universe."[4]

a. *Jesus' faithful love*

The revelation of Yahweh's faithful love is the heart of the Old Testament, the heart of the covenant. There already, the psalmist sings: "For his great love ("hesed") is without end" (Ps 107:1; see 118:1-4; and especially Ps 136). Still, the Mosaic covenant was not the definitive revelation of God's love, and the Old Testament itself opens up to a new covenant. Moreover, notwithstanding the moving texts of the prophets about Yahweh's tender and faithful love, it was eventually understood in a very defective way. In Judaism, a legal mentality predominated in the end, and the Law, fragmented in so many precepts, smothered love, says Fr. Arrupe.

It was in the mission of his Son, that the full depth of Yahweh's love was revealed in a definitive way. In him, God has committed himself for ever, not just to Israel, but to mankind. "God's love for us was revealed when God sent into the world his only Son . . ." (1 Jn 4:9).

The definitive character of God's love for us was revealed in the very fact of the Incarnation: Jesus, herald of the Father's love; Jesus, incarnation of the Father's love. It was revealed even more clearly in the way Jesus lived and died for us: "God did not spare his own Son, but gave him up to benefit us all" (Rm 8:32). Jesus came, as bridegroom (Jn 3:29); as the Good Shepherd (Jn 10:14) who even gave his life for his sheep (Jn 10:15). "A man can have no greater love than to lay down his life for his friends" (Jn 15:13). "I have loved them as much as you loved me" (Jn 17:23).

The letter to the Hebrews stresses the "once for all" character ("ephapax") of Jesus' mediation, which ensures the eternity of the new covenant: "the blood that sealed an eternal covenant" (Heb 13:20). The old covenant was imperfect, because it remained on the level of shadows and figures; the new covenant is perfect, because Jesus our High Priest assures us of everlasting access to the presence of God (Heb 10:19). For ever and ever, God is now our God, and we are his people. "Nothing therefore can come between us and the love of Christ . . ." (Rm 8:35-39).

b. The universality of Jesus' love

Jesus' love is radically new, because it transcends and abolishes the limitations and restrictions which narrowed down the idea of love in the Old Testament. Lv 19:18 does prescribe: "Love your neighbor as yourself," but "Who is my neighbor?" In the Old Testament it was thought that only members of one's own people, of one's own faith, were neighbors. "Christ breaks down the fences of a restricted brotherhood, and this is his great revolution of love: universal salvation, universal filiation, universal brotherhood, and universal love, are all correlative ideas, logically connected and interchangeable" (Arrupe, op. cit., p. 104). The notion "neighbor" is masterfully reinterpreted in the parable of the Good Samaritan (Lk 10:29-37).

Even enemies are not excluded: "But I say to you: love your enemies, and pray for those who persecute you. In this way you will be sons of your Father in heaven, for he causes his sun to rise on bad men as well as good, and his rain to fall on honest and dishonest men alike" (Mt 5:43-48). The universality of the Father's love is now clearly revealed, and it becomes the norm of our love. In Jesus' view, tribalism is out; racism is out; sexism is out, for we are all brothers and sisters. Even though his personal ministry was limited to Israel, he sends his disciples to go and teach all nations, till the end of time. His special concern for the sinners, the sick, the poor, the outcast, will be treated next in a special section.

c. *A compassionate love. Jesus' mercy*

There was a tendency in the Old Testament to affirm one's piety by declaring one's hatred for sinners. Jesus did not do this: he came to call, "not the virtuous, but the sinners" (Mk 2:17). He surprised many by forgiving sins, by eating with publicans and sinners (Mk 2:15-16). We all remember his exquisite tact in dealing with the adulterous woman (Jn 8:3-11). With one question he was able to silence a crowd ready to stone her. St. Mary Magdalene became his friend; so did Matthew and Zacchaeus. He even called Judas his friend, and asked forgiveness for the ones crucifying him. By his merciful love he was able to heal people, and to bring out the best in them. Pope John Paul II opens his beautiful encyclical *Dives in Misericordia* with the quotation of Ep 2:4-5: "But God loved us with so much love that he was generous with his mercy: when we were dead through our sins, he brought us to life with Christ — it is through grace that you have been saved — and raised us up with him." Is this not exactly the meaning of the gracious love of God of which Christ is the incarnation ("He who sees me, sees the Father"): that he saves us from our misery, that he heals the brokenhearted, that he seeks what was lost?

The idea of pardoning the sinner is central in Jesus' ministry. Peter noticed it (Mt 18:21), and asked: "Lord, how often must I forgive my brother if he wrongs me? As often as seven times?" But Peter was still counting; Jesus was not: "Not seven, I tell you, but seventy-seven times." There is no limit to mercy. Jesus came, not as judge, but as savior (Jn 3:17; 12:47). He is the lamb that takes away the sins of the world (Jn 1:29), and he shed his blood for the remission of sins (Mt 26:28). Love is redemptive, for love cares.

This same concern that Jesus showed towards spiritual misery he felt towards people in all kinds of other misery: the sick, the outcast, the poor, the hungry. I do not think that we express this concern sufficiently when we say that Jesus "loved all people, including the sick, the poor. . . ." There is more to it: is there not a certain preference, a "preferential option," for these groups? And does this not follow from the very nature of compassionate love? President Kennedy said in his first presidential speech: "Those who have less in life, should have more in law." The compassionate person feels: those who have less in life, have a greater right to be loved. That is but fair; it can even be a most urgent necessity.

After the publication of the documents of Medellin and Puebla the "preferential option for the poor" received much attention. Such an option is clearly rooted in the very nature of God as revealed in the Scriptures: Yahweh hears the cry of the poor. In response to this cry, another cry can be heard as well from the Scriptures, a cry from the very Heart of God: "You do not care for the poor? I do!" The Church must be the incarnation of that cry, as Jesus was. We are not excused; the compassionate person cannot pass by "on the other side of the road" (Lk 10:31), but makes himself neighbor.

To see Jesus' mercy in action, we have to look at the miracle stories: Jesus healing the sick, raising the dead, feeding the hungry crowd, changing water into wine. We have to look at Jesus, forgiving sins, having dinner with the publicans and sinners, talking with women (even this, it seems, was unusual). A group of texts that reveal Jesus' compassionate Heart very clearly and that add a psychological touch are those mentioning that when Jesus *saw* the misery of people, he was moved with compassion: Mt 9:36; Lk 7:13; 10:33; 15:20; Jn 11:33.

We also have to reflect on certain sayings of Jesus: "What I want is mercy, not sacrifice" (Mt 9:13). "Blessed are the poor" (Lk 6:20-21). And on certain parables: the parable of choosing guests to be invited (Lk 14:12-14); the parable of the unforgiving debtor (Mt 18:23-35); the parable of the lost sheep, the lost drachma, and, above all, the parable of the prodigal son (all these three in Lk 15). These parables make us think of God as the merciful Father, and of Jesus as the Good Samaritan, as he is the Good Shepherd who goes after the lost sheep. Jesus the Good Samaritan: healing the wounds of ailing mankind, and paying the price. Jesus the suffering Servant. His answer to the disciples of John the Baptist really sums up his ministry and characterizes him as the one who was to come (Lk 7:18-23). Here you have the sign of authenticity: merciful love in action. Here the new heart is revealed.

d. His Hour

Jesus' whole life was a revelation of love for the Father and for us, but during the last twenty-four hours he outdid himself. His last will and testament, his farewell gifts, are so impressive and unforgettable that I would like to consider them separately. Two places require our attention: the cenacle, where he had his Last Supper, and Calvary, where he was crucified. St. John needs seven chapters to narrate what happened on the last day.

"He had always loved those who were his in the world, but now he showed how perfect his love was" (Jn 13:1). Jesus did not have a stone to lay his head on, so it would seem that his last will and testament would be a simple affair. Instead, he bequeathed us a large number of most exquisite gifts. The Last

Supper opened with the washing of the feet. Before giving us his new commandment of love by word of mouth, he wanted to give a personal example to make it clear what kind of love he had in mind: a love that serves; a love that shows itself in the little services of every day. That comes first. He was about to lay down his life for us, the ultimate gift. But he had time for this little act, to exemplify his "mandatum."

At this stage, the Synoptists speak of another action of Jesus, the institution of the Holy Eucharist: "Do this in memory of me." The ideal farewell gift that sums up his preaching on the Kingdom: communion, fraternal sharing of bread, giving oneself. It explains the meaning of his death too: "my blood, poured out for you." It is a gift that enables him to remain present in our midst in a very real way: "He who eats my flesh and drinks my blood, remains in me and I in him." That is the ideal farewell gift.

Having thus manifested his love in action, he gives us *his* commandment: "My little children, I shall not be with you much longer. . . . I give you a new commandment: love one another; just as I have loved you, you also must love one another" (Jn 13:33-35). In Lv 19:18, the Israelites were told: "You must love your neighbor as yourself." Jesus' commandment is new, for "just as I have loved you" raises this commandment to new, incomprehensible heights. It is this love that "fulfills" the law and the prophets, surpassing them by far. A little later, Jesus explains the meaning of "just as I have loved you": he really means the love of "Abba": "As the Father has loved me, so I have loved you" (Jn 15:9). No wonder that St. John can say that "Anyone who lives in love, lives in God" (1 Jn 4:16), for all authentic love comes from God, whose essence is love.

Besides these two unforgettable gifts, the Eucharist and his commandment, Jesus gave us his friendship too: "I shall not call you servants any more . . . I call you friends, because I have made known to you everything I have learnt from my Father" (Jn 15:14-15). He gave us his final warnings regarding a loveless world (Jn 16:1-4); he gave us the promise of the spiritual presence in our hearts of the Father, of the Son, and of the Holy Spirit (Jn 14:23). Especially the promise of the Spirit is developed several times: Jn 14:26; 15:26; 16:7-15. Jesus will send him; the Spirit is his gift, to lead us into the whole truth. Here we have the promise of another most precious gift.

The farewell meal ends with Jesus' priestly prayer (Jn 17). Here he gives us his prayer. He asks the Father to consecrate us in truth, to give us eternal life, to make us perfectly one, and, as his last request: "that the love with which you loved me may be in them, and so that I may be in them."

The moment of his death is the other culminating point. It was a moment of few words. He gave forgiveness, even to the ones who crucified him. He gave us his mother, for whom, like the beloved disciple, we may make a place in our home: "This is your mother." And he entrusted us to her. And when all was accomplished, he gave his life: "He gave up his spirit." Jesus did not have a stone to lay his head on; he had nothing; he gave us everything. He emptied himself. Such is love.

5. *Jesus, gentle and humble of Heart (Mt 11:25-30)*[5]

When studying Jesus' Heart in the New Testament one can certainly not bypass the one text in the gospels where Jesus' Heart is explicitly mentioned (Mt 11:29), all the more so since Jesus gives us here the reason why we should become his disciples. In fact, we have here a very rich text but, as in the case of some other rich texts, it is not so simple to point out its richness in a few words. When we want to explain Jesus' words spoken during the Last Supper: "This cup is the new covenant in my blood," we cannot possibly do that without referring to Moses who said: "This is the blood of the covenant," and without referring to Calvary where Jesus shed his blood in fact. Similarly we cannot explain this short passage of Matthew, without referring to quite a number of other biblical passages, to realize what Jesus really means.

To understand the three verses of Mt 11:28-30, we must place them in their context. They are part of a larger whole, Mt 11:25-30, a passage that is called "the Hymn of Jubilation." In Matthew, the introduction of this hymn is solemn: "At that time Jesus exclaimed: 'I bless you, Father, Lord of heaven and of earth. . . .' " In the parallel text of Luke, the introduction is even more solemn and joyful: "It was then that, filled with joy by the Holy Spirit, he said, 'I bless you, Father, Lord of heaven and of earth . . .' " (Lk 10:21-22). Evidently, there is good reason to speak of a "Hymn of Jubilation." We find here Jesus' Heart, filled with admiration and gratitude for the ways of his Father.

Analyzing the pericope, we find that, in Matthew, it consists of three logia of our Lord, which, it seems to me, form a real unit:

1 — Mt 11:25-26:

Jesus blessed the Father for revealing the mysteries of the Kingdom, not to the wise, but to the little ones. Note that in Mt 13:11 it is said that these mysteries are revealed to the Apostles.

2 — Mt 11:27:

The mutual knowledge logion.

3 — Mt 11:28-30:

The invitation to discipleship, or: the teacher with the light yoke. The first two logia are found in the parallel text of Lk 10:21-22; the third one, however, is not. I would now like to comment on the second and third logia of Matthew, for they require further explanation.

Mt 11:27-30:

The second and third logia have many ramifications in Scripture.

a. *Ramifications in sapiential texts*

In the first place, they evoke several *sapiential texts*. By way of introduction, look at Mt 11:19 where Jesus himself refers to Wisdom, and compares himself with it. When we look at Pr 8:22-36 (esp. vv. 32-35), at Si 24 (esp. v. 24) and at Ws 9:9-18, we see that in these three texts Wisdom presents herself as having a deep knowledge of things divine, and as inviting people to come and listen to her. In our Matthean passage, Jesus presents himself as having a unique knowledge of the Father (v. 27), and as inviting people to come to him (vv. 28-30). This Old Testament background shows the connection between the second and third logia. In the Old Testament, Wisdom speaks as personified; here in Matthew, Jesus speaks as a true person, Wisdom in person, the unique Son of God. In fact, the text presents Jesus as the unique Son of Man as well, for the words "Everything has been entrusted to me by my Father" evoke the Son of Man text of Dn 7:14. Jesus presents himself here as the Wisdom of God, arranging everything. Also linguistically the relationship of Mt 11:27-30 with some Wisdom texts can be shown. In Si 51:26-27 ("place your neck under her yoke") we find four typical words that occur also here in Matthew: yoke, labor, find, peace. Something similar can be said of Si 6:24-28.

b. *Ramifications in Johannine texts*

Secondly, this Matthean passage evokes several *Johannine texts*, a reason why this pericope is often called "the Johannine passage." Compare Jn 1:18, 3:11 and 6:46 where Jesus speaks of his unique knowledge of the Father. And Jn 6:35, 37, 67; 7:37 where Jesus says: "Come to me." In John, Jesus is the revelation of the Father because he is the Word of God incarnate, "the only Son who is nearest to the Father's Heart" (Jn 1:18). In Matthew, Jesus is divine Wisdom in human form; the Son who knows God as no one else does; the only one really who can reveal the Father, to those whom he chooses.

c. *The third logion (Mt 11:28-30)*

"Shoulder my yoke and become my disciples, for I am gentle and humble of heart." The words "gentle and humble" belong to the biblical tradition of the poor of Yahweh. They are · the opposite of rich, proud people who go their own way, thinking they don't need God. In 2 Cor 10:1 St. Paul uses these same two words: the gentleness of Christ, the humility of Paul's behavior in Corinth. In Col 3:12 he mentions both again in a context that does justice to the saying of St. John Chrysostom: "the heart of Paul is the Heart of Christ." "You should be clothed in sincere compassion, in kindness and *humility, gentleness* and patience. Bear with one another; forgive each other. . . ."

In the Old Testament, these two terms occur together for the first time in Zp 3:12, referring to poor people (in Hebrew: "ani" and "dal"); they occur also in Is 26:6. In the Psalms too they refer to the simple, poor people who trust in God:

— Ps 34 (33):
   salvation is promised to the humble, the brokenhearted.
— Ps 25 (24):9:
   says that Yahweh teaches the humble and the poor.
— Ps 37 (36):11:
   says that the gentle (Jerusalm Bible: the humble)
   shall possess the land.

From these psalms it appears that there is not much difference in meaning between the two terms "gentle" and "humble"; several times "gentle" is translated by "humble." Both refer to an attitude of deep respect for God, on whom we depend and without whom we know that we can achieve nothing. In the Beatitudes Jesus has a distinct reference to the poor in spirit, and to the gentle. But, as is well known, the poor, the hungry, the gentle, the persecuted, all belong to the same class of people: the anawim. They are blessed; Jesus preaches to them, and the Kingdom is theirs. It is all summed up in Is 61:1-2, quoted in Lk 4:18.

From these references it becomes clear that when Jesus says that he is gentle and humble of heart, he places himself among the poor of Yahweh. He presents himself as one of the anawim, as belonging to them, not only by his external poverty, but even more so by the dispositions of his heart.

Now we are in a position to look at the marvel of the whole passage: Jesus, the Wisdom of God, the unique Son of the Father, the glorious Son of Man, is at the same time one of the poor of Yahweh, one of those humble, dependent people. He is gentle and humble of heart, not proud, but completely subject to God, the ideal example of the poor in spirit. That is why he can invite the poor people, all those who labor and are heavy burdened, to come to him, for he is one of them.

Glorious and poor; great and humble. To understand something of this paradox we have to consider that Jesus is the Logos incarnate, the unique Son of God who became one of us. And he was humbler yet: he became one of the poor, in a poor town. He has nothing of himself; he is really poor; whatever he has, is the Father's gift. So he is at home with the poor people.

In fact, he is the humble "Servant of Yahweh." Isaiah 42:1-4 (the first Song of the Servant) is applied to him in Matthew's next chapter: 12:18-21. He is the one who is kind to the downtrodden; who "does not break the crushed reed, nor put out the smoldering wick." He brings true peace. By his suffering he cures the many.

Jesus' solidarity with the poor is rooted in his heart. He feels like them, simple, unassuming; he belongs to them. Here we see the connection with the first logion: the Kingdom of God is for the little ones, for to them God reveals himself. So Jesus invites them: "Come to me. . . ." What a unique Teacher: divine in wisdom; most human in his approach. He speaks from experience, for he was poor himself. He is most concerned about the ones he has to teach; able to give rest to their souls. May we be small enough to become his disciples. Blessed be the Father, for giving us such a Teacher, who knows him as no other and who feels with us, poor people, as no other. In his Heart are all the treasures of wisdom and knowledge; in his Heart are the feelings of a gentle, helpful Servant, eager to assist, to enlighten, to lighten our burden, to heal our restless souls with his peace.

ART. 2
JESUS' HEART, A PASCHAL AND PENTECOSTAL MYSTERY

Having reflected on Jesus' Heart in terms of his deepest concerns and attitudes, we must now consider the Johannine doctrine of Jesus' Heart, source of living water, and the opening of that source by the piercing of his side with the lance. Historically, this was the oldest theology of the Sacred Heart, developed by the Fathers, as shown by the Rahner brothers. I will not explain here the difficulty with Jn 7:37-38, solved by Hugo Rahner (see Chapter 7, art. 1,1), but will limit myself to the biblical theology of this mystery. [6]

1. The source of living water (Jn 7:37-39)

> On the last day and greatest day of the festival, Jesus stood there and cried out: "If any man is thirsty, let him come to me! Let the man come and drink — who believes in me!" As Scripture says: From his breast shall flow fountains of living water.
> He was speaking of the Spirit which those who believed in him were to receive; for there was no Spirit as yet because Jesus had not yet been glorified.

This text brings us to Jerusalem, at the time of the celebration of the feast of Tabernacles. During that feast water, drawn from the well at Siloe, was carried in procession to the Temple, and on the seventh day it was poured around the altar. It was an occasion of prayer for rain, but at the same time the pilgrims recalled the blessings of the early years in the desert: how Moses had given them water by striking the rock, an event that Isaiah already had transformed into a sign of messianic salvation: "You will draw water joyfully from the springs of salvation" (Is 12:3; compare Ps 36:9).

It was at that occasion that Jesus presented himself as the source of living water. As he had invited those who labor and are heavy burdened to find rest (Mt 11:28) so here he invites those who are thirsty, those who believe in him, to drink. See also Rv 22:1, 17.

For as Scripture says, "From his breast shall flow fountains of living water." This text is not found literally in the Old Testament; closest to it, maybe, comes Ps 78:16: "conjuring streams from the rock, and bringing down water in torrents." But the *idea* that the messianic times will be characterized by a rich outpouring of the Spirit, and the idea of symbolizing the gift of the Spirit by the image of water, even of living water, is common in the Old Testament.

We already know the beautiful text of Ezekiel 36:27: "I shall put my spirit in you," a promise given in the context of the renewal of our hearts. We are also familiar with the idea that the Messiah (i.e. the "Anointed One") will be full of the Spirit: "On him the spirit of Yahweh rests: a spirit of wisdom and insight . . ." (Is 11:1-9); and Is 61:1: "The spirit of the Lord Yahweh has been given to me, for Yahweh has anointed me . . ." (quoted in Lk 4:18 where Jesus applies the text to himself).

The Spirit is the eschatological gift that sums up salvation, that brings the fullness of life, as water brings dry land to life. Isaiah already compares water and spirit: "For I will pour out water on the thirsty soil, streams on the dry ground. I will pour out my spirit on your descendants, my blessings on your children." A beautiful text too is Ezk 47:1-12, which describes a mysterious stream flowing from the midst of the Temple, from near the altar, and bringing fertility and abundance of life wherever it reaches. Rv 22:1 is clearly a reference to this text: the crystal-clear river of life flowing down the middle of the city street in the heavenly Jerusalem. Also Zc 14:8 mentions: "When that day comes, running waters will come from Jerusalem. . . ." For the expression "living water" see also Jr 2:13.

Early Christianity had already identified Christ and the rock from which water flowed (see 1 Cor 10:4): "For the rock was Christ." And Jesus himself identified his risen body with the Temple (Jn 2:19). In this way we have here a rich theology of Jesus, source of living water, source of the Spirit. What is new in John is that he refers to Jesus' "interior" (koilia) as the source. From this source we can drink by believing, and Jesus invites us to do so.

Jesus, the Anointed One, will become the source of the Spirit for us when he will be glorified. In his talk with the Samaritan woman (Jn 4:14) he had already spoken of living water that he alone can give, and there he says that this living water will turn into a spring inside the believer, welling up to eternal life. Thus the heart of the believer too is a source of the Spirit, who gradually transforms the whole person. But in John 7 Jesus affirms that he himself will become the source of the Spirit *for others*, for all believers, for "from his fullness we have all of us received" (Jn 1:16). Note how the whole of this theology is an argument for the "Ephesian" reading of Jn 7:37-38 which makes Jesus the source of living water.

Here we find Jesus' Heart as redemptive mystery, as the source of the new life for all of us, and we are invited to approach in faith, and drink. We need not go as far as saying that before Jesus' glorification the Holy Spirit was never given; also in the Old Testament we see people moved by the Spirit of God. But what is new in messianic times is the richness of the outpouring of the Spirit, whom Jesus is eager to send. In St. John, Jesus' first paschal act on the evening of the first day of Easter is to communicate the Spirit: "Receive the Holy Spirit" (Jn 20:22).

2. The pierced Heart (Jn 19:31-37)

One of the soldiers pierced his side with a lance, and immediately there came out blood and water.

All was accomplished: ". . . and bowing his head he gave up his spirit" (Jn 19:30). But then, something else happened. A "postscriptum" to Jesus' life and death, the piercing of his side. For the executioners, a mere act of making sure that Jesus of Nazareth was dead, but for St. John, a significant event to which he testifies in a most solemn way (vv. 35-37). Jesus' legs were not broken, for Jesus is the paschal lamb (Ex 12:46). Moreover Zc 12:10 had mysteriously foretold that "they will look on the one whom they have pierced," in a context of "pouring out a spirit of kindness and prayer" (Zc 12:10), and "opening up a fountain for the House of David and the citizens of Jerusalem" (Zc 13:1). St. John saw this fulfilled here.

This is significant. If the piercing of Jesus' side, with the flowing of blood and water, is the fulfillment of this text of Zechariah, then this means that it is the fulfillment of the whole prophetic tradition about the messianic gift of living water, of the Spirit; that it is the fulfillment, somehow, of Jn 7:37-39, as the Fathers believed. The Spirit was to be given after Jesus' glorification, but St. John presents the crucifixion as a being "lifted up," in other words, as the beginning of the glorification. And the flowing of blood and water becomes in this context an important sign of the communication of the Spirit. The source has been opened, and starts flowing. When we now look in faith upon the one whom they have pierced, we shall be healed by the life-giving Spirit.

Blood and water: the sacrificial blood; the water that symbolizes the Spirit. The Fathers go further and think of the sacraments: Eucharist and Baptism; the Church, formed from Jesus' side as the new Eve. The medieval mystics looked upon the one whom they have pierced and discovered Jesus' loving Heart. Each generation is invited to look at the pierced one, and ponder the mystery. Here we are at the source; those who are thirsty are invited to drink. And the life-giving Spirit will become a source in us, in our hearts, gradually transforming our lives, gradually renewing us and our world.

This is a paschal mystery, a mystery of death and new

life. It is a pentecostal mystery, a mystery of the outpouring of the Spirit. Here we discover that the paschal and pentecostal mystery is the center of the spirituality of the heart. Here we start to realize how Yahweh fulfills his promise of giving us a new heart: through the blood shed on the cross; through the Spirit who leads us into the whole truth and who, according to St. Paul, teaches us to love. It is good to stay at the source, where the water is crystal clear, and look. And drink. "Send forth your Spirit and they shall be created, and you shall renew the face of the earth" (Ps 104:30).

Notes

1. In the first part of this chapter I relied on the important article of I. de la Potterie, S.J., "Fondement Biblique de la Théologie du Coeur du Christ." in Card. Ciappi et. al., *Le Coeur de Jésus, Coeur du Monde*. FAC ed. 1982, pp. 103-140. Subsequently, this article was included in de la Potterie's book: *Il Mistero del Cuore Trafitto. Fondamenti biblici della Spiritualità del Cuore di Gesù*. EDB 1988.
2. Jesus' experience of the Spirit has been treated theologically in the book of James D.G. Dunn, *Jesus and the Spirit*. S.C.M. Press 1975.
3. I. de la Potterie, in Ciappi, op. cit., 113-121.
4. Fr. Arrupe's article is contained in E.J. Cuskelly, M.S.C., *With a Human Heart*, 92-119, and also in Pedro Arrupe, S.J., *In Him alone is our Hope. Reflections on the Heart of Christ*. Manila 1984.
5. Special bibliography about Mt 11:25-30:
   E.J. Cuskelly, M.S.C., *A New Heart and a New Spirit*, pp. 37-47.
   A. Feuillet, S.J., "I fondamenti del Culto al Cuore di Gesù secondo il NT," in *Il Cuore di Gesù e la Teologia Cattolica*. Ed. Dehoniane 1965, pp. 138-148.
   H. Mertens, *L'Hymne de Jubilation chez les Synoptiques: Mt 11:25-30 et Lc 10:21-22*. Gembloux 1957.
   Note that even at present the scholars do not agree on the exact translation of Mt 11:29. The English Jerusalem Bible has: "Shoulder my yoke and learn from me *for* I am gentle . . .", while the Italian and Spanish Jerusalem Bibles translate: "learn from me *that* I am gentle . . ." The Greek text uses the word "hoti," the primary meaning of which is "that"; in some cases, however, it can mean "because." Personally I think that in this context it means "because," for Jesus seems to be giving a reason why we should shoulder *his* yoke and become his disciples. A third possibility is the translation of the Dutch Willibrord Bible (1975): "Learn from me: I am gentle . . ."; this covers both meanings of "hoti."

6. An important contribution to the study of Jn 7:37-38 was made by Hugo Rahner, "Flumina de ventre Jesu. Die patristiche Auslegung von Johannes 7:37-38" in *Biblica* 22, 1940, 269-302; 367-403. In line with this study I accept the "Ephesian" reading of Jn 7:37-38 which makes Jesus the source of living water. See further Hugo Rahner, "On the Biblical Basis of the Devotion." in J. Stierli, *Heart of the Savior*, pp. 15-35.

Alfred Carminati, S.C.J., *E venuto nell'Aqua e nel Sangue. Riflessione Biblico-Patristica.* Ed. Dehoniane, Bologna 1979.

J.F. Lescrauwaet, M.S.C., *Triptych for a Spirituality of the Heart*, 1975.

E. Malatesta, S.J., and Jesus Solano, S.J., *The Heart of Christ and the Heart of Man.* Roma 1978 (ad usum privatum) 9-20.

CHAPTER FIVE

THE RENEWAL OF OUR HEART
ACCORDING TO THE NEW TESTAMENT

The term "heart" occurs 159 times in the New Testament. Three of these texts are however commonly rejected by the text critics (Lk 4:18; 5:21 and Ac 8:37). One time the term refers to the Heart of God (Ac 13:22), and one time to the heart of the earth (Mt 12:40). That leaves a total of 154 texts using the term with reference to the human heart. Let us see whether we find here the fulfillment of God's promise about the new heart. [1]

1. The importance of the heart in Jesus' teaching

When we study Jesus' message, it becomes clear that he aimed at nothing less than a deep transformation of the person. This is shown also by the fact that he frequently used the term "heart." In Matthew, we find the term 16 times, always on the lips of Jesus himself. I will use Matthew's gospel to show how important the renewal of heart is according to Jesus. [2]

a. The beatitudes

There is a striking contrast between the ten commandments and the beatitudes. As the ten commandments occupy the central place in the law given on Mount Sinai, so the beatitudes occupy the first place in the Sermon on the Mount. The ten commandments are mostly concerned with well-defined actions, whereas the beatitudes express what the Christian is, the basic attitudes of mind and heart, poverty in spirit, purity of heart, etc.

b. Moral impurity and ritual impurity

Jesus' concern with what makes a person really upright, with the dispositions of the heart, is revealed strikingly in his reply to the Pharisees who attacked him because his disciples did not perform the ritual washing of hands before the meals (Mt 15:1-20). In this reply Jesus refers not only to ritual washings but also to the custom of considering some kinds of food "unclean."

First he accuses the Pharisees of breaking away from the divine commandments for the sake of their traditions. He calls them hypocrites, and quotes the strong text of Is 29:13:

> This people honors me only with lip-service,
> while their hearts are far from me.
> The worship they offer me is worthless;
> the doctrines they teach are only human regulations.

Then Jesus explains his own view: "What goes into the mouth does not make a man unclean; it is what comes out of the mouth that makes him unclean" (Mt 15:11). "The things that come out of the mouth come from the heart, and it is these that make a man unclean. For from the heart come evil intentions, murder, adultery . . ." (Mt 15:19). Mark 7:19 remarks: "Thus he pronounced all foods clean." Jesus was not interested in certain traditions about ritual purity; he is interested in a pure heart.

c. Interiorization of the law

One section of the Sermon on the Mount makes an explicit contrast between the old and the new law (Mt 5:21-48). The contrast consists primarily in that the new law goes deeper; it reaches out to the heart. Not only is killing wrong, but also hating one's brother; not only is adultery wrong, but also the unchaste desire, the "adultery of the heart" (Mt 5:28). With regard to the Jewish classical triad of good works, almsgiving, prayer and fasting, Jesus is concerned with the right motivation, lest they become an external show.

The deepening of the new morality is also revealed in the two points Jesus makes in Mt 5:38-48, points which are characteristic of the new heart. The first point is the abolition of "vendetta." The Jewish law of retribution, "Eye for eye, and tooth for tooth," was in fact universal practice in the world at large. It was tribal law in so many countries: a member of a clan is killed, so some one of the killer's clan must be killed; and there is no end to this vicious circle. Jesus brings the solution: forgiveness, nonviolence. Vendetta is unchristian.

The second point (Mt 15:43-48) concerns the universality of the commandment of brotherly love. No one is excluded, not even our enemies. The universal love of the heavenly Father is the norm. For Jesus, the sun that shines for everybody is a beautiful symbol of the universality of the love he preached.

d. The principle

Jesus aims at renewal of heart; when the heart is good, good actions will follow: "How can your speech be good when you are evil? For a man's words flow out of what fills his heart. A good man draws good things from his store of goodness; a bad man draws bad things from his store of badness" (Mt 12:33-37). The same principle is found in Mt 7:17-18: "A sound tree cannot bear bad fruit, nor a rotten tree good fruit."

Our actions spring from what we are; the heart is the source. That is why it is so important that our heart be set on authentic values: "Where your treasure is, there your heart is, too" (Mt 6:21). In our chapter on Jesus' Heart we have seen what his basic values were: the Father, the will of the Father, the Kingdom, love and mercy, being gentle and humble of heart, etc. To enter the Kingdom, to be Jesus' disciples, we certainly need a deep conversion, a metanoia, a new heart.

2. *"Hearts, purified by faith" (Ac 15:9)*

In the traditional devotion to the Sacred Heart, we were accustomed to pay attention to the love of Christ which kindles our love. This remains, of course, central; still it is surprising how many texts we find in the New Testament about the role of faith in the renewal of our heart. A quick count gave me a total of 47 verses referring to the heart in connection with faith. The process of conversion starts with faith: "Be converted, and believe the Good News" (Mk 1:15). Conversion starts with the acceptance of Jesus, for he is the way; he is the healer who brings new life.

a. *The obstacles to faith: a closed heart*

> Then, grieved to find them so obstinate (lit. "grieved about the obstinacy of their heart"), he looked angrily round at them. (Mk 3:5)

The lack of faith Jesus encountered during his public life is a frequent theme in the New Testament, and several times this is traced to the heart (Mk 2:8; Mt 9:4). Even the apostles were not free from this attitude, for Mk 6:52 says: "Their minds (lit. "hearts") were closed." The letter to the Hebrews refers twice to Psalm 95:8: "If only you would listen to him today, 'Do not harden your hearts as at Meribah. . . .'" See Heb 3:7; 3:15.

St. Stephen was even more direct. In Ac 7:51 he tells the Sanhedrin: "You stubborn people, with your pagan hearts and pagan ears. You are always resisting the Holy Spirit, just as your ancestors used to do." Ac 7:54 describes the reaction of the Sanhedrin: "They were infuriated (lit. "in their hearts") when they heard this, and ground their teeth at him." In Ac 7:39 he mentions another defect of the heart in connection with faith: lack of perseverance, of fidelity. Speaking of Moses he says: "This is the man that our ancestors refused to listen to: they pushed him aside, turned back to Egypt in their thoughts (lit. "in their hearts"). . . ." They had started the journey to the promised land, but in their hearts they turned back to Egypt, thinking of the food they had enjoyed there. The hardships of the journey gave them second thoughts, and their idealism faltered. Regarding a wavering faith, James 4:8 says: "Clear your minds (lit. "your hearts"), you waverers."

St. Paul too refers several times to difficulties arising from the heart and preventing people to believe "from the heart" (Rm 6:17). See Ep 4:18; Rm 1:21; 1:24; 2:5. Interesting is the image he uses in 2 Cor 3:15: Moses' face was covered with a veil, but even now a veil covers the hearts of the Israelites. "Yes, even today, whenever Moses is read, the veil is over their minds (lit. "over their hearts"). It will not be removed until they turn to the Lord." Only after turning to the Lord can we, with unveiled faces, reflect the brightness of the Lord.

b. The process of faith

Jesus has shown us our real vocation: human brotherhood, God as Father, citizens of the Kingdom. But our aspirations are too low; we are too selfish; we too often live in fear. We have no idea of what this world could be, of what God has in store for us. "The hidden wisdom of God which we teach in our mysteries," says St. Paul in 1 Cor 2:7-9, "is the wisdom that God predestined to be for our glory before the ages began. . . . We teach what Scripture calls: 'the things that no eye has seen and no ear has heard,' things beyond the mind (lit. "the heart") of man, all that God has prepared for those who love him." To realize our vocation, to bring about the new heavens and the new earth, we have to share Jesus' vision of the Father and of the Kingdom. Our hearts must be "purified by faith," says St. Peter in Ac 15:9, purified of our narrow, selfish vision by the wisdom of God, by his Word, and by the pure light of his Spirit. For it is by these two agents that God carries out his promise to give us a new heart: by his Word and his Spirit.

The first step in the process of faith is the opening of the heart. When God addresses his word to us, we must not only listen with our ears but also with the heart. But to be able to do that is a gift of God. St. Luke tells us in Ac 16:14 that Lydia "listened to us, and the Lord opened her heart to accept what Paul was saying." Everybody can listen with his ears when the word is addressed to him; but to be "cut to the heart" (Ac 2:37), as those Jews on the day of Pentecost, is a grace of God.

A listening heart, a receptive heart. In the parable of the sower, some seeds fall in rich soil: "These are people with a noble and generous heart, who have heard the word, and take it to themselves, and yield a harvest through perseverance" (Lk 8:15). The true disciples,the true kinsmen of Jesus, not only hear the word, they also "keep" it (Lk 11:28), and "put it into practice" (Lk 8:21). This last text includes the Virgin Mary, the first believer, the first disciple. Her prayerful heart is mentioned twice in Luke: "As for Mary, she treasured all these things, and pondered them in her heart" (Lk 2:19; cf. 2:52).

This is an important aspect of true discipleship: hearing the word, receiving it, keeping it in the heart, pondering it, and putting it into practice. The last step, the practice, presupposes previous contemplation, a life of prayer, of pondering the word. In the one text of the gospels which explicitly mentions the Heart of Christ, he invites us to become his disciples and learn from him, for he is gentle and humble of heart (Mt 11:29). He is the teacher who can set our hearts afire, as when he explained the Scriptures to the disciples at Emmaus, whose hearts were burning (Lk 24:32). If we are thirsty, if we believe in him, we must come to him, to drink from the living water he alone can give, for his Heart is the source of the Spirit (Jn 3:38ff). The acceptance of Christ leads to the acceptance of the Spirit of Christ, who becomes a source in us, welling up to eternal life (Jn 4:14).

c. *The indwelling Word*

The doctrine of the role of faith as the primary factor in the process of conversion, of renewal of heart, has been marvelously developed by St. Paul. The work of purifying our hearts starts with the grace of illumination. "It is the same God that said: 'Let there be light shining out of darkness,' who has shone in our hearts to radiate the light of the knowledge of God's glory, the glory on the face of Christ" (2 Cor 4:6; compare 2 P 1:19). As the process of creation started with "Let there be light," so the process of the recreation of our hearts starts with letting the light of God's glory penetrate our hearts, the light that Jesus brought into the world, for he said: "I am the light of the world." Once there is light, we can see what remains to be done. When we look at ourselves and at our world in the light of faith, we realize that much is to be done to make God's Kingdom come.

In the act of faith St. Paul distinguishes two aspects: the external confession, and the acceptance with the heart. In the following text he mentions the heart three times:

> The word, that is the faith we proclaim, is very near to you, it is on your lips and in your heart. If your lips confess that Jesus is Lord and if you believe in your heart that God has raised him from the dead, then you will be saved. By believing from the heart you are made righteous; by confessing with your lips you are saved.
>
> (Rm 10:8-10)

Both aspects are important: believing with the heart, and confessing with the lips, the internal and the external. Still it should be stressed that faith is not a mere external confession, but primarily an attitude of the heart, a personal surrender to Christ, an acceptance of Christ together with his message. The word that we believe in is in fact the divine Word incarnate, and so faith becomes a union with Christ. It is not just "the word" that is kept and pondered in the heart, but Jesus himself, the Word, comes to live in our heart, and that changes everything. This is marvelously expressed in a prayer of St. Paul that sums up the whole spirituality of the heart in one mighty sentence:

> Out of his infinite glory, may he give you the power
> through his Spirit for your hidden self to grow strong, so
> that Christ may live in your hearts through faith, and
> then, planted in love and built on love, you will with all
> the saints have strength to grasp the breadth and the
> length, the height and the depth; until, knowing the love
> of Christ, which is beyond all knowledge, you are filled
> with the utter fullness of God. (Ep 3:16-19)

Through faith, Christ lives in our hearts. From a market
place, our heart becomes a temple. He strengthens us in the
Church, and makes us grasp the depth of God's plan, the scope
of his love, and leads us into the utter fullness of God.

In the same letter we find another prayer of St. Paul, a
prayer for the faithful at Ephesus, in which he describes the
activity of the Father in the process of faith:

> May the God of our Lord Jesus Christ, the Father of glory,
> give you a spirit of wisdom and perception of what is
> revealed, to bring you to full knowledge of him. May he
> enlighten the eyes of your mind (lit. "your heart") so that
> you can see what hope his call holds for you, what rich
> glories he has promised the saints will inherit and how
> infinitely great is the power that he has exercised for us
> believers. (Ep 1:17-19; compare 1 Cor 4:5)

"May he enlighten the eyes of your heart." In the light of
Christ, the Father makes us see in a new way; we start to share
Jesus' vision of the Father and of the Kingdom, the Father's
glorious plan. Vision comes first, and this puts everything in a
new context; this opens the way to hope and to confidence in
God's power. The way of faith is a way of purification, of
illumination, and of union with the indwelling Word.

d. The indwelling Spirit

Faith is supposed to be living and growing, and in this
process the Holy Spirit has an essential role. This has been
described by St. John and St. Paul.

St. John narrates that Jesus promised us the Holy Spirit: "I shall ask the Father, and he will give you another Advocate, to be with you for ever, the Spirit of truth. . . . You know him, because he is with you, he is in you" (Jn 14:16-17). "The Advocate, the Holy Spirit, whom the Father will send in my name, will teach you everything and remind you of all I have said to you" (Jn 14:26). "He will lead you to the complete truth" (Jn 16:13).

Acts 2 narrates one glorious instance of the fulfillment of this promise: the outpouring of the Holy Spirit on Pentecost day. This passage shows that the Holy Spirit gives not only light, but also courage and power to proclaim our faith openly, and that by this preaching of the word people can be "cut to the heart" (Ac 2:37). The Holy Spirit is at work, not only in those who preach but also in those who listen. He brings the whole Church to life.

That the heart is the "place" where the Spirit dwells is often taught by St. Paul, for example in 2 Cor 1:22:

> Remember it is God himself who assures us all, and you,
> of our standing in Christ, and has anointed us, marking
> us with his seal and giving us the pledge, the Spirit, that
> we carry in our hearts.

Life in the Spirit is most beautifully described in Romans 8. "The Spirit of God has made his home in you" (Rm 8:9). He is the new law written in our hearts: "The law of the Spirit of life in Christ Jesus has set us free from the law of sin and death" (Rm 8:2). Now we must learn to live according to that new law. "Everyone moved by the Spirit is a son of God. The Spirit you received is not the spirit of slaves bringing fear into our lives again; it is the Spirit of sons, and it makes us cry out, 'Abba, Father!' " (Rm 8:15; compare Gal 4:6). The Spirit makes us pray the way Jesus prayed; he teaches us to relate to God the way Jesus did. Then St. Paul goes on to describe how the whole of creation groans to share in the liberation from fear and death, to give birth to the new heavens and the new earth. As

God's Spirit hovered over the waters at the beginning of creation, as the same Spirit brought Adam to life, so the Spirit of God, the Spirit of the new Adam, brings us and the whole of creation to new life. As sin comes from the heart, so liberation starts from the heart in which the Spirit dwells, for where the Spirit is, there is freedom. The Spirit, who knows the depths of God, guides the process of renewal along the lines revealed by God's Word. The renewal must first be revealed and lived in the human heart before the universe can be renewed.

3. "The love of God has been poured into our hearts" (Rm 5:5)

Jesus went around preaching that the process of renewal starts with new vision, with faith, with discipleship, with turning to Christ who gives us his paschal gift, the Holy Spirit.

But Jesus' great and new commandment is love: love with all the new dimensions treated in the previous chapter, a faithful, universal and merciful love. This theme has been beautifully treated by St. John, the beloved disciple, and by St. Paul who gave us the hymn of love (1 Cor 13). I cannot do full justice to this great theme here; I intend to treat the texts about the heart. But I did find 11 heart-texts in the New Testament that speak of love.

a. The first commandment of the Lord

> This is the first: "Listen, Israel, the Lord our God is the one Lord, and you must love the Lord your God with all your heart, with all your soul, with all your mind and with all your strength." The second is this: "You must love your neighbor as yourself." There is no commandment greater than these.
>
> (Mk 12:29-30)

Matthew 22:40 adds:

On these two commandments hang the whole Law, and
the prophets also. (Compare Lk 10:27 and Mk 12:33.)

Though the formulation of these two commandments has
been taken from the Old Testament, much about them is new.
In the first place, "the second commandment" has been promoted next to the first, so that the two of them form, in fact, one
commandment of love. In Jn 13:34 the stress on brotherly love
is even more striking: "I give you a new commandment: Love
one another. Just as I have loved you, you also must love one
another."

The second deep change in these two commandments is
that both have been transformed in Jesus' heart: the "love of
God" becomes "love of Abba," hence a new intimacy, a new
way of relating to God. And love of neighbor has been
deepened by Jesus' conception of "neighbor," as explained in
the parable of the Good Samaritan (Lk 10:29-37). Further-
more, there is Jesus' new stress on forgiveness and compassion. "And that is how my heavenly Father will deal with you
unless you each forgive your brother from your heart" (Mt
18:35).

b. *The Spirit of love*

The new law is clearly a law of love, for that sums up
everything. We have said above that the Spirit is the new law
written in our heart. And this blends well with love as the new
law, for the Holy Spirit is not merely the Spirit of truth, but also
the Spirit of love. "The love of God has been poured into our
hearts by the Holy Spirit which has been given us" (Rm 5:5).

Note the last part of this quotation: "by the Holy Spirit
which has been given us." The Holy Spirit moves our hearts to
love, not as an external agent, but from within. As the Spirit of
sonship, he teaches us to live as sons and daughters of God; he
teaches us to address God as "Abba," and to love him as
"Abba." In 2 Th 3:5 St. Paul prays: "May the Lord turn your
hearts towards the love of God and the fortitude of Christ." This

the Lord Jesus Christ does, not just by his example, but even more so by his Spirit.

The same Holy Spirit moves us also to love our brothers and sisters. As the "soul" of the mystical body of Christ, he makes us one, and moves each member to serve the whole body. By his charisms he enables us all to serve, each in our own way. After Pentecost, "The whole group of believers was united, heart and soul; no one claimed for his own use anything that he had, as everything they owned was held in common" (Ac 4:32).

The love inspired by the Holy Spirit is a practical love; it opens up a whole new program of love: forgiveness, mercy, sharing, service. The oneness of heart and soul of the first Christian community was the fulfillment of the promise of Jr 32:37-41 about the "singleness of heart." The "one heart" includes unity of faith, but evidently also unity of love: they shared their property in common.

When treating the role of faith, I mentioned the obstacles to faith: obstinacy and doubting. Love also has its own obstacles. 2 P 2:14 mentions: "Greed is the one lesson their minds (lit. "their hearts") have learnt." Our hearts are selfish; we are not ready to share. The great sacrament Jesus left us as his memorial is the breaking of the Bread together. But that is exactly the one thing we seem to be unable to learn; so many are starving; our hearts are not yet new.

St. Paul had the spirit of the first Christian community; he organized a big collection to support the poor in Jerusalem (2 Cor 8:6-15). In 2 Cor 9:7 he says: "Each one should give what he has decided in his own mind (lit. "in his own heart"), not grudgingly or because he is made to, for God loves a cheerful giver." And 1 P 1:22: "You have been obedient to the truth and purified your souls until you can love like brothers, in sincerity; let your love for each other be real and from the heart — your new birth was not from any mortal seed but from the everlasting word of the living and eternal God."

The new life is a sharing in the life of Christ by faith, hope and love. By faith Christ enters into our hearts; he sends his

Spirit who makes us pray "Abba." The Spirit moves us to love, and where there is love, there is hope. This is called the "spiritual life," not because it is lived exclusively on the level of our spiritual faculties, but because it is a life "in the Spirit." To give food to the hungry is "a spiritual act" when it is inspired by the Holy Spirit.

> Send forth your Spirit and they shall be created,
> and You shall renew the face of the earth.

4. *"In your minds you must be the same as Christ Jesus" (Ph 2:5)*

Christ came to bring us new life, and St. Paul saw the consequences. In Ep 4:22-24 he writes:

> You must give up your old way of life; you must put aside your old self, which gets corrupted by following illusory desires. Your mind must be renewed by a spiritual re-volution, so that you can put on the new self that has been created in God's way, in the goodness and holiness of the truth.

In Gal 3:27 he summarizes this program of renewal in one simple expression: "All baptized in Christ, you have all clothed yourselves in Christ." And what this means is spelled out again in greater detail in Ph 2:1-5:

> If our life in Christ means anything to you, if love can persuade at all, or the Spirit that we have in common, or any tenderness and sympathy, then be united in your convictions and united in your love, with a common purpose and a common mind. That is the one thing which would make me completely happy. There must be no competition among you, no conceit; but everybody is to be self-effacing. Always consider the other person to be better than yourself, so that nobody thinks of his own

interest first but everybody thinks of other people's interests instead. In your minds you must be the same as
Christ Jesus.

This passage sums up, in the first place, what we have
already considered in this chapter: unity of faith and love in
Christ. But then Paul mentions some further consequences of
life in Christ: no competition, to be self-effacing, etc. Here we
may think of the gentleness and humility of Christ the Servant.
In all these sentiments of Christ we are meant to share. To
become a Christian means to let our hearts be conformed with
the Heart of Christ. We cannot work this out in detail, but the
typical "heart-texts" should be quoted here.

We have already referred to Romans 8, where St. Paul
explains what life in the Spirit means: a transition from death to
life, a spirit of sonship, justification, groaning in the Spirit,
and the liberation of the whole cosmos. Quite a program! In the
second part of many of his letters, St. Paul gives some practical
guidelines, conclusions from "being in Christ." The substance
of the law was already engraved in our hearts as a natural gift
(see Rm 2:15). When we are reborn of water and Spirit, the law
of Christ is engraved in our hearts, and the Spirit inspires us
from within to live the new life. This requires, as a first
consequence, that we must learn to listen to the Holy Spirit.
When we pray, when we listen to people, the Spirit has a way to
make us realize what we should do. Let us now study in detail
what the New Testament teaches about the new heart.

a. God knows our hearts

In the first place there are a number of texts stating that
God knows the heart, a doctrine already common in the Old
Testament. See Lk 16:15; Ac 8:21; Rm 8:27; 1 Th 2:4; Rv
2:23.

Luke (9:47) mentions that *Jesus* knew the thoughts that
were going on in the hearts of his apostles. In 1 Cor 14:25 Paul
says that the people who have a special charism of the Holy

Spirit may be able to reveal the thoughts of the heart of someone else.

To express God's ability to read our hearts a special term was coined: "Kardiognostès," "the one who knows the hearts" (Ac 1:24 and 15:8).

b. *The Lord Jesus confirms our hearts*

> May the Lord be generous in increasing your love and make you love one another and the whole human race as much as we love you. And may he so confirm your hearts in holiness that you may be blameless in the sight of our God and Father when our Lord Jesus Christ comes with all his saints. (1 Th 3:12-13).

> May our Lord Jesus Christ himself, and God our Father who has given us his love and, through his grace, such inexhaustible comfort and such sure hope, comfort you (lit. "your heart") and strengthen you in everything good that you do or say. (2 Th 2:16-17)

c. *Purity of heart*

The pure of heart were called blessed by our Lord (Mt 5:8); they shall see God. Pure of heart are those whose heart is undefiled and undivided. They shall see God. Not only in heaven but also here on earth, they are better attuned to the will of God and to his gracious design. They are mentioned again in 2 Tm 2:22:

> Instead of giving in to your impulses like a young man, fasten your attention on holiness, faith, love and peace, in union with all those who call on the Lord with pure minds (lit. "with pure hearts"; cf. Heb 10:22).

d. *Beauty should come from within*

Women should not dress up for show; they should rather dress their hearts with a gentle disposition. 1 P 3:3-5:

Do not dress up for show; doing up your hair, wearing
gold bracelets and fine clothes; all this should be inside,
in a person's heart, imperishable: the ornament of a sweet
and gentle disposition — this is what is precious in the
sight of God.

e. The new heart is a sincere heart

So as we go in let us be sincere in heart and filled with
faith, our minds (lit. "our hearts") sprinkled and free
from any trace of bad conscience and our bodies washed
with pure water. (Heb 10:22)

f. Simplicity of heart

Close to sincerity and truthfulness is simplicity of heart.
Twice St. Paul exhorts slaves to obey their masters "with
simplicity of heart"; in Col 3:22, where the Jerusalem Bible
translates "wholeheartedly"; and in Ep 6:5 where it translates
"with sincere loyalty." The expression occurs also in Ac 2:46:
the first Christian community "shared their food gladly and
generously (lit. "with simplicity of heart")."

In all three cases "simplicity of heart" means without
pretense, sincerely. Fraternal sharing and obedience must be
sincere; spirituality of the heart is essentially "sincere." A
simple heart is the opposite of duplicity, of a divided heart, of a
divided loyalty.

g. Reverencing Christ in our heart

"Simply reverence the Lord Christ in your hearts" (1 P
3:15).

The fact that Christ dwells in our heart opens the way to
intimate contact with him. We can speak to him, listen to him,
worship him, love him who lives in our heart. In Ezekiel we
met three times the expression "They have enshrined their own
idols in their heart" (Ezk 14:3; 14:4; 14:7). But rather than

enshrine idols in one's heart, one can also enshrine the Lord Jesus in one's heart, and let him be Lord there.

h. Gratitude, joy and peace

As we share in the new life of Christ, our hearts should not be troubled (Jn 14:1; 14:27b). They should rather be full of peace: "And may the peace of Christ reign in your hearts, because it is for this that you were called together as parts of one body" (Col 3:15; compare Ph 4:7).

Our hearts should be full of paschal joy (Ac 2:26; Jn 16:22) and we should be singing in our hearts:

> Sing the words and tunes of the psalms and hymns when you are together, and go on singing and chanting to the Lord in your hearts, so that always and everywhere you are giving thanks to God who is our Father in the name of our Lord Jesus Christ. (Ep 5:19-20)

The new heart is a grateful heart: "With gratitude in your hearts sing psalms and hymns and inspired songs to God, and never say or do anything except in the name of the Lord Jesus, giving thanks to God the Father through him" (Col 3:16).

i. The new heart is faithful

Faithfulness is a basic attitude of the new heart. Our faith and love must be faithful, for the new covenant is an eternal covenant. This idea is expressed in a variety of ways. Acts 11:23 states:

> The church in Jerusalem heard about this and they sent Barnabas to Antioch. There he could see for himself that God had given grace, and this pleased him, and he urged them all to remain faithful to the Lord with heartfelt devotion (lit. "to persevere in the proposition of the heart").

Yahweh's heart has been revealed to us as faithful to the covenant; his great love is without end. He made a new covenant to prepare himself a responsive and faithful people, faithful servants, as Jesus was faithful, "unto death." Only a faithful marriage (Mt 19:1-9) can be a true sign of the new covenant. When St. John says that Jesus was full of "grace and truth" (Jn 1:14), he refers to an Old Testament expression, "hesed we emet," which means: faithful love, mercy and fidelity. From that fullness we have received, and so we must "remain" in his love (Jn 15:9). True love is faithful. It seems that in our time faithfulness is in crisis once more. The spirituality of the heart must foster faithfulness.

j. God is greater than our heart

> My children, our love is not to be just words or mere talk, but something real and active; only by this can we be certain that we are children of the truth and be able to quieten our conscience (lit. "our heart") in his presence, whatever accusations it may raise against us, because God is greater than our conscience (lit. "our heart") and he knows everything. My dear people, if we cannot be condemned by our own conscience (lit. "our own heart"), we need not be afraid in God's presence, and whatever we ask him, we shall receive, because we keep his commandments and live the kind of life that he wants. (1 Jn 3:18-22)

In this passage, St. John mentions the heart four times; it is an important text. Whatever accusation our heart may raise against us, we may rest secure before God if our love is real and active. When we are guided by true love, we need not be afraid, and God will hear our prayer. Sure, there will be shortcomings, but "God is greater than our heart." His mercy transcends ours; his faithfulness transcends ours and heals our fickleness. He understands us better than we understand ourselves.

This passage is written in a context about love. St. John

assures us that when we walk the path of neighborly love, we live in God who is love.

> This has taught us love: that he gave his life for us; and we, too, ought to give up our lives for our brothers. If a man who was rich enough in this world's goods saw that one of his brothers was in need, but closed his heart to him, how could the love of God be living in him? (1 Jn 3:16-17)

5. *The heart of an apostle*

The spirituality of the heart is essentially a missionary spirituality. Jesus, the new Adam, shared with us his vision of the Father and of the glorious plan of the Father, the Kingdom. From his pierced Heart the Church was born, and Jesus' Spirit inspires the Church to continue Jesus' mission of love. When our hearts are renewed by Jesus' vision and love, we cannot but burn with desire to renew society. He who loves cannot let his brothers and sisters suffer. As Jesus' love was redemptive, so must our love be. As Jesus' mission was to serve, so must our mission be. As the Good Shepherd cares for the lost sheep, so must we. As Jesus came to heal the brokenhearted, so must we, for we have been anointed by his Spirit.

Jesus was very much aware of being sent by someone else: by the Father. Still his mission was "interiorized" to such an extent that what he said and did came also very much from his own Heart. He believed in what he preached and in what he did. We, in turn, are sent by him, and our mission too must come from within, from the heart. St. Peter and St. John stated in front of the Sanhedrin that they could not stop proclaiming what they had heard and seen: "We cannot but speak!" (Ac 4:20). They were compelled from within, to carry out their mission. It is important that we too are moved by our own heart, to speak and to act. We cannot touch hearts if our own heart has not been touched. We cannot heal hearts that are broken if we have not experienced the healing touch of grace ourselves, even though we will always be "wounded healers." We cannot assist people to enter into the depths of their hearts, to listen to the Word and to let themselves be moved by the indwelling Spirit, if we have not entered ourselves into this mystery. Only a burning heart can kindle a flame.

All this we find beautifully exemplified in the life and in the words of St. Paul. Many texts refer to his apostolic heart, and these texts illustrate how the mission can be carried out "from the heart."

a. St. Paul's apostolic heart

A first group of "heart-texts" express St. Paul's great love and deep concern for his own people:

> What I want to say is this: my sorrow is so great, my mental anguish (lit. "the continuous anguish in my heart") so endless, I would willingly be condemned and be cut off from Christ if it could help my brothers of Israel, my own flesh and blood. (Rm 9:2)

> Brothers, I have the very warmest love (lit. "love in my heart") for the Jews, and I pray to God for them to be saved. (Rm 10:1)

As a Christian and as an apostle St. Paul differed deeply from the majority of his own people; still he continued loving them. He did not reject his roots. This too is important for our missionaries, when their home countries develop in ways they cannot understand.

Equally tender and strong were his feelings for the Christian communities he founded, and he does not hesitate to express these feelings:

> When I wrote to you, in deep distress and anguish of mind (lit. "of heart"), and in tears, it was not to make you feel hurt but to let you know how much love I have for you.
> (2 Cor 2:4)

> Corinthians, we have spoken to you very frankly; our mind (lit. "our heart") has been opened in front of you.
> (2 Cor 6:11)

I am not saying this to put any blame on you; as I have already told you, you are in our hearts — together we live or together we die. (2 Cor 7:3)

Only one who loves strongly can speak as frankly as St. Paul and be accepted. His love is realistic and faithful. These texts remind us of the passionate "anger-texts" about Yahweh's Heart. Paul had the warmest feelings especially for the Philippians.

It is only natural that I should feel like this towards you all, since you have shared the privileges which have been mine: both my chains and my work defending and establishing the gospel. You have a permanent place in my heart, and God knows how much I miss you all, loving you as Christ Jesus loves you. (Ph 1:7)

Already in his first letter he expresses such feelings:

A short time after we had been separated from you — in body but never in thought (lit. "in heart"), brothers — we had an especially strong desire and longing to see you face to face again, and we tried hard to come and visit you. (1 Th 2:17)

St. Paul's pastoral love was also returned, but this did not diminish his freedom to carry out his mission elsewhere:

When we heard this, we and everybody there implored Paul not to go on to Jerusalem. To this he replied, "What are you trying to do — weaken my resolution (lit. "weaken my heart") by your tears? For my part, I am ready not only to be tied up but even to die in Jerusalem for the name of the Lord Jesus." (Ac 21:13)

Finally, he was able to inspire this same pastoral concern in the hearts of his fellow-workers:

I thank God for putting into Titus' heart the same concern for you that I have myself. (2 Cor 8:16)

This, too, is an important point: to build up pastoral teams that are truly inspired. He was able to work with men and women, and for himself he chose the celibate life, to be completely free for his mission.

b. Heart speaks to heart

Another set of Pauline "heart-texts" speak of the purpose of his mission, a mission that is primarily directed at the heart of the faithful.

> It is all to bind you together in love and to stir your minds (lit. "hearts"), so that your understanding may come to full development, until you really know God's secret in which all the jewels of wisdom and knowledge are hidden. (Col 2:2)

> The only purpose of this instruction is that there should be love, coming out of a pure heart, a clean conscience and a sincere faith. (1 Tm 1:5)

This last text sums up very well what we found in this chapter: the Christian message aims at a pure heart renewed by faith and love, and by a lifestyle inspired by love.

Twice Paul mentions that he sent a minister to a local church "to strengthen their hearts":

> I am sending him to you precisely for this purpose, to give you news about us and to reassure you (lit. "to strengthen your hearts"). (Ep 6:22; see Col 4:8)

The heart of Paul, says St. John Chrysostom, was the Heart of Christ. The new law was written in his heart, as Jeremiah and Ezekiel had announced, and by his missionary dedication the Holy Spirit wrote the same letter in the hearts of his flock.

> Unlike other people, we need no letters of recommendation either to you or from you, because you are yourselves

our letter, written in our hearts, that anybody can see and read, and it is plain that you are a letter from Christ, drawn up by us, and written not with ink but with the Spirit of the living God, not on stone tablets but on the tablets of your living hearts. (2 Cor 3:1-3)

This completes our biblical synthesis of the spirituality of the heart: God fulfills his promise to renew our hearts by his Word and by his Spirit, and in this process the Church has a role. Like St. Paul, the ministers of the Church (and this includes all ministries) assist in drawing up what is to be written on the hearts of the believers. Parents, teachers, ministers of the Word, we are all sent to contribute to the renewal of heart of those we meet. All Christians are meant to be like a tree planted on the borders of the mysterious stream of living water, producing fruit in all seasons; "and the leaves of which are the cure for the nations" (Ps 1:3 together with Rv 22:2).

> Now I am making the whole of creation new . . .
> I will give water from the well of life free
> to anybody who is thirsty. (Rv 21:5-6)

Notes

1. Some bibliography:
   G. Kittel, *Grande Lessico del Nuovo Testamento*, s.v. "kardia."
   A. Diez-Macho, M.S.C., "The Heart in the Bible. Symbol of the Person." in E.J.Cuskelly, M.S.C., *With a Human Heart*, pp. 42-68.
   E. Malatesta, S.J. and Jesùs Solano, S.J., *The Heart of Christ and the Heart of Man.* Rome 1978.
2. For this study of St. Matthew's gospel I have used the article by L. Dunlop, "Christ Model of 'Religion of the Heart.' " in E.J. Cuskelly, *With a Human Heart*, pp. 27-33. *Ibid.*, see the articles of John Flynn and Thomas A. Kane.

CHAPTER SIX

THE SPIRITUALITY OF THE HEART AND OUR LADY

The study of the spirituality of the heart would be incomplete if we did not mention the important place of our Lady in this spirituality. The Church has recognized at least two devotions to our Lady which are relevant here: the devotion to the Immaculate Heart of Mary (Mass on the Saturday after the feast of the Sacred Heart), and, in the society to which I belong, the devotion to our Lady of the Sacred Heart (Mass on the last Saturday of May, proper to several religious societies).

The first of these devotions concerns Mary's heart considered in itself; the second looks at Mary as related to the Sacred Heart of her Son. Both devotions are related to the renewal of our heart, in their own way. I am not concerned here with the history of these devotions, but I would like to consider what we can say about them from a scriptural point of view.

1. The Immaculate Heart of Mary

The phrase "the Immaculate Heart of Mary" makes us think of Mary's sinless heart or, more positively, of her pure heart, her gracious heart ("Rejoice, O highly favored!" Lk 1:28). Biblically one might prefer to speak of her prayerful heart, for the two texts that mention her heart explicitly (Lk 2:19 and 51) speak of Mary storing in her heart all that concerns her Son, treasuring and pondering these things in her heart. Here we find the heart of the first believer, the first disciple, who makes rapid progress in the knowledge of her Son, who ponders the mystery of her Son to whom she dedicates her whole life.

From this prayerful heart welled up so many prayers, six of which were noted down in the gospels. A short meditation on these prayers will teach us something about Mary's gracious heart.

"But how can this come about, since I am a virgin?" (Lk 1:34)

This is a prayer for instruction, addressed to the angel Gabriel during the annunciation. Mary asks for light concerning her mission.

"I am the handmaid of the Lord, let what you have said be done to me." (Lk 1:38)

Here we meet Mary's humble and obedient heart: the heart of a servant, ready to do what God asks from her. The attitude expressed here is strikingly similar to the attitude of God's Son, expressed in his prayer "on coming into the world . . .: 'God, here I am! I am coming to obey your will.' " (Heb 10:4-7). Jesus' prayer was the prayer of our High Priest who takes the place of the sacrifices of the Old Testament. Mary too soon learned that as Jesus' Mother she would have to suffer: "A sword will pierce your own soul too . . ." (Lk 2:35).

"My child, why have you done this to us? See how worried your father and I have been, looking for you." (Lk 2:48)

These are the first words of Mary addressed to Jesus that are known to us. They are a motherly complaint about Jesus' behavior. Mary did not understand why Jesus went his own way without informing them. Jesus' answer did not remove the mystery but deepened it: he had to busy himself with his Father's affairs. Jesus has another Father, whose will must prevail. Mary must have pondered this word often. She started to realize that Jesus could not always do what she would like. Jesus increased in wisdom. So did Mary.

"They have no wine." (Jn 2:3)

Again a prayer addressed to her Son. It is not a mere statement, a mere observation. Jesus understands that his Mother wants him to do something about it. This prayer reveals Mary's caring heart; she notices needs and intercedes with her Son, with motherly confidence.

"Do whatever he tells you." (Jn 2:5)

Mary's advice to the servants. This too reveals Mary's faith and confidence in her Son. If we may take this word of our Lady in a wider sense and look at them as directed to all servants of the Lord, it is the best lesson our Lady gives us: "Do whatever he tells you."

"My soul proclaims the greatness of the Lord . . ." (Lk 1:46-55)

Mary opens her heart most fully in her Magnificat, her song of admiration and praise for the great things the Lord has done to her personally and to Abraham and his descendants. She admires the greatness and power of the Almighty, and adores his Holy Name. Like her Son, she is aware of God's predilection for the little ones: Yahweh routs the proud of heart and exalts the lowly; he fills the hungry with good things and sends the rich away empty. Here we notice the accents of Jesus' beatitudes. Mary has a deep insight in the nature of God's redeeming love, his "hesed," his mercy. Twice she refers to it, in vv. 50 and 55. God's love is such that he redeems those who suffer: the lowly, the hungry, the true children of Abraham. St. John Eudes liked to say that Mary and Jesus have only one heart. The Magnificat proves it.

2. *Our Lady of the Sacred Heart*

The two devotions referred to above partially overlap. We cannot speak of Mary's heart without looking at her faith in and love for her Son, for he was her great love, her life. But the devotion to our Lady of the Sacred Heart brings this relationship with her Son directly into focus. The object of the first and older devotion is Mary's heart; the object of the second is a relationship, in fact the most beautiful human relationship ever.

Relations are very important; psychology teaches that relations are essential for personal development. Insofar as they are mother and son, the relationship between Jesus and Mary is unique: only she was his mother. But at the same time they present a model: the relationship between the new Adam and the new Eve. I would like to distinguish two dimensions in their relationship: their personal communion, and their association in Jesus' mission.

a. *The relationship of Jesus and Mary on the level of their personal life*

"Hail, full of grace" (Lk 1:28).

In all relations in which God is involved, the initiative comes from the side of God. The first words directed to Mary in Scripture are: "Hail, full of grace," or, more literally: "Rejoice, O highly favored." From the beginning of her existence Mary was highly favored, loved, chosen, prepared for her mission, and made most gracious by God. Guided by the Spirit, she continued to grow as Daughter of Sion, so that because of her we can say that the stage was set for the birth of the Messiah.

"Fiat!" (Lk 1:38)

When Mary was invited to become the Mother of the Messiah, she was ready: "Behold the handmaid of the Lord. Be it done to me. . . ." Her fiat was the acceptance of her calling and mission. It was the expression of her commitment to be Jesus' Mother. And as Jesus' life unfolded, her commitment continued to grow, for at first it was far from clear what was involved.

Virgin-Mother

When Jesus was born, Mary dedicated herself to him with her whole heart. It is beautiful to think that Mary and Joseph together decided to live a virginal life for the sake of this child, so that their virginity has a christological significance: they were the first two Christian virgins. Jesus was their greatest love and concern; he was the central meaning of their lives. If we may understand Mary's virginity in this way, it set her free for her function to be Jesus' Mother.

Motherhood far transcends the biological level. Mary gave Jesus his humanity: through Mary, Jesus was enabled to become the incarnation of divine love. Mary taught him to love. She had an important role in Jesus' human development in all aspects, including the religious aspect. It was from her that Jesus learned to pray to his heavenly Father. Before Mary became Jesus' disciple, Jesus was first the disciple of Mary. In fact, in a sense they owed each other everything.

It was Mary's privilege and joy to discover the perfection of Jesus' heart: his gracious love, his obedience, his growing awareness of the Father, his awakening passion for the Kingdom of his Father. And when the time came for Jesus to start his public life, our Lady was ready; by then she understood that he had to be concerned with the things of his Father.

Only glimpses have been revealed of Jesus' hidden life, and of Mary's life with him. Most attention is given to her faith: "Blessed is she who believed!" (Lk 1:45). Since she pondered in her heart whatever she learned about her Son, her faith grew marvelously, and she obtained an intimate knowledge of the mystery of her Son. It is mentioned that she wondered at the things that were said about him (Lk 2:33), that she was worried when she lost him in Jerusalem (Lk 2:48), and that she could not understand why he stayed behind without telling his parents. There was darkness too in her life. It is mentioned that Jesus lived under their authority (Lk 2:51).

During his public life Jesus twice revealed his admiration for his mother's faith: "Still happier those who hear the word of God and keep it" (Lk 11:28; compare Lk 8:21). He esteemed Mary more highly for her faith than for being his mother. She truly belonged to his new family as mother, the mother of our faith (Lk 8:21). The more her faith developed, the deeper their communion became; their relationship was a growing thing.

b. Mary's association with Jesus in his mission

What we have said so far about our Lady (her fiat, her faith, her virginal motherhood) prepared the ground for the next step: her involvement in Jesus' mission, her cooperation in the work of redemption. Mary is not only Jesus' Mother, she was and is also his associate. So we have to reflect now on her partnership with her Son in his redemptive task, for that too is part of the mystery of her relationship, her union with him.

1. The new Eve

People have often wondered about the fact that Jesus addressed his mother sometimes as "Woman." Though it was customary at that time to address a woman that way, it was not customary for a son to address his mother with that title. At Cana Jesus said: "Woman, why turn to me? My hour has not come yet" (Jn 2:4). And on Calvary: "Woman, this is your son" (Jn 19:26).

I think that we can find the key to the solution of that problem in another work from the Johannine circle, Rv 12. There we read about "a woman, adorned with the sun, standing on the moon, and with twelve stars on her head for a crown. She was pregnant and in labor," while a huge red dragon was waiting to snatch the child from her. The child that is born is clearly the Messiah.

This vision is an enlarged version of the proto-gospel (Gn 3:15): "I will make you enemies of each other, you and *the woman*, your offspring and her offspring. It will crush your head and you will strike its heel." These words were addressed to Eve and the Tempter. Jesus is the offspring of the woman that crushes the Tempter's head; Mary is the woman, the new Eve, who shares in the victory. It is true that the woman in Rv 12 refers primarily to Mother Church, as the exegetes explain, but a secondary, Mariological sense is not to be excluded, as Raymond Brown holds. Here, in fact, we find Mary as the archetype of Mother Church. She is the new Woman, the new Eve, sharing in Jesus' sufferings, sharing in his victory, as Eve had shared in the fall.

Jesus and Mary: the new Adam and the new Eve. That is the mystery of Mary's title "Woman." As the first Adam and Eve were the source of our broken human existence, so the new Adam and the new Eve are the source of the new life in the Spirit. They were closely united in their personal life; they were also closely united in the paschal mystery, in the redemption of the world, in the outpouring of the Spirit. As Jesus was the Servant of the Lord, so was Mary the Handmaid of the Lord, ready to obey, to serve, and to suffer.

2. *Mary's sufferings*

It was Simeon who first pointed out to Mary that she would have to suffer: "He is destined for the fall and for the resurrection of many in Israel, destined to be a sign that is rejected — and a sword will pierce your own soul too — " (Lk 2:34-35). The general context of this suffering seems to be the rejection of her Son. She must have experienced his rejection deeply during the last year of Jesus' public life, but the culminating point came when she stood beneath the cross, united with him in his sufferings. If Jesus had to learn obedience through suffering, so had Mary. By her faithfulness, her strength, her suffering and her prayer, she became the Mother of the Church. Her prayerful heart had to be pierced, to be a worthy companion of the Man with the pierced Heart.

3. Mother and Archetype of the Church

Mary's divine motherhood developed into universal motherhood. In a sense she is already the mother of us all because she gave Christ to the world. But that is not all. She was associated as well with her Son in his work of redemption, in his epiphany, in his obedience, in his sufferings. And by her prayer she obtained for us the gift of the Holy Spirit who brought the Church to life.

Vatican II has developed the idea that in all this Mary is the archetype of the Church (*Lumen Gentium* art. 63-65). The Church too is our Mother, obtaining for us the gift of the Spirit, especially in baptism and confirmation. The Church too is the new Eve, born from the side of the new Adam when he slept on the cross. From Mary, the Church can learn how to remain closely united with the Lord in her mission, how to be the Mother of the faithful, how to praise the Lord, and how to serve the poor. From Mary, the Church must learn how to be the new Eve, how to live in close union with Christ in complete dedication as virgin-mother; how to suffer with him, to work with him, to obtain the gift of the Spirit from him.

Now what is true of the Church as such is somewhat true also of the individual members of the Church. All Christians are called to learn from her to enter personally into a life of close union with Christ, to look upon the one whom they have pierced, to share his mission of renewing the world by love.

4. Sharing Jesus' Lordship

We believe that our Lady continues to live in union with her Son after her Assumption. She continues to love him as her Son; she shares in his Lordship as Queen; she shares in his intercession as Mediatrix. That is why we continue to pray to her.

But it is good to note Mary's path to this glory in the Scriptures: the way of the humble Handmaid of Nazareth, the unadorned picture of Mary the first believer and faithful disciple, the suffering Mother. The knowledge of her continued presence now gives us hope and strength; the knowledge of her courageous and gracious life on earth shows the way. Her life on earth was not glorious according to secular standards, but most glorious in the eyes of God.

From Our Lady of the Sacred Heart we learn to live in union with her Son: in personal communion, and in association with his mission. From her we learn to accept our calling and mission generously, and to remain faithful when the cross appears. Sharing the mystery of her union with her Son, we will come to know the source of living water that renews the world.

5. *The triptych of Our Lady of the Sacred Heart*

For the first proper Mass of Our Lady of the Sacred Heart, approved in 1925, the passage of Jn 2:1-11, the marriage feast at Cana, was chosen as the gospel. In the new Mass, approved in 1972, the gospel is Jn 19:25-37: Mary beneath the cross, given to us as Mother, and looking at the one whom they have pierced. It occurred to me that there is another important text about Mary's involvement in the paschal mystery, namely Ac 1:14: Mary, praying with the apostles in the cenacle, and obtaining by her prayer the abundant outpouring of the Spirit. This text could well be used as the key to the other two, and the three texts together give us an insight in Mary's role in the spirituality of the heart: the triptych of Our Lady of the Sacred Heart, with Mary beneath the cross as central panel.

At Calvary, Mary saw the opening of Jesus' side, and the blood and water that flowed from it. This passage must be read in conjunction with Jn 7:37-39: "If any man is thirsty, let him come to me; let him drink, who believes in me." This, says St. John, Jesus said of the Spirit. At Calvary, the source of living water was opened, and Mary witnessed it. But not only that: she participated in the mystery of redemption on a very deep level. She gave moral support to her Son by her presence, and she suffered with him, so that Jesus was able to point to her as our Mother: "Behold your Mother." This moment was the culminating point of their association and union.

At Cana, Mary obtained from Jesus the gift of wine for the marriage feast. This was a prefiguration: the abundance of new wine is a sign of the abundant outpouring of the Spirit, promised for the new covenant. Mary had a role in obtaining this gift; she interceded with faith and confidence.

Here Mary reveals herself as the first believer. The apostles started to believe as a consequence of this first sign, but Mary already believed before the sign was given. The beginning faith of the apostles marks the start of the messianic marriage feast. The Church begins to be united with the Bridegroom. We notice Mary's role in the epiphany of Jesus: he manifests his glory at her insistence.

In the Cenacle, Mary joined the apostles in prayer during the first pentecostal novena, and she obtained the rich outpouring of the Spirit. This is the time of fulfillment, the completion of the paschal mystery. Jesus shares his new life with us, and Mary, our Mother, remains associated with him. Here we see our Lady in action as Mother of the Church, bringing the Church to life by obtaining the gift of the Spirit, of which the Heart of her Son is the Source. She was there when the faith of the disciples started; she was there when the disciples became courageous apostles. And in both instances she had a hand in their growth.

It is on this note that the biblical story of our Lady ends. What she did in the cenacle, she continues to do in heaven, for all disciples of Jesus. She remains associated with the mystery of Jesus' Heart, obtaining for all disciples the gift of faith in her Son, the gift of love, for she obtains for them Jesus' paschal gift of the Spirit. She is the true woman at the well, able to draw living water, to renew our hearts. Her closeness to her Son enables her to lead us to the source.

CHAPTER SEVEN

THE HEART IN CHRISTIAN TRADITION

The devotion to the Sacred Heart as it was practiced in the Catholic Church during the last few centuries was closely linked to the revelations granted to St. Margaret Mary Alacoque. The theologians, however, have always known that a devotion is never based on private revelation; the true foundation is to be found in Christian revelation as handed on by the apostles.

A study of the true foundation can be very useful: it may show what is basic in a devotion, and what are personal accents. Of course we do not intend to take away anything from the merit of St. Margaret Mary; she remains the beloved disciple and the great apostle of the Sacred Heart. She gave great impetus to the devotion, and the liturgical celebration of the feast of the Sacred Heart as approved for the whole Church was a fruit of her request.

Much has been written already on the history of this devotion: first on St. Margaret Mary and St. John Eudes, then on the period immediately preceding them, especially on the devotion in the middle ages. Still later it was discovered that the Fathers of the Church already speak of Jesus' side, and of his Heart. Recently also the wider topic of the human heart in Christian writing and in the liturgy has been investigated.

Thus we are now able to present a new synthesis: the spirituality of the heart in Christian tradition. This is an immense topic, and I do not intend to develop it here at great length. But having presented a biblical synthesis of the spirituality of the heart it may be useful to add at least an outline of this theme, with a few important quotations, to show how it developed in tradition.

ART. 1   THE PATRISTIC ERA

K. Richstatter, the great specialist of the Sacred Heart devotion in the middle ages, wrote: "In the first thousand years of Christianity, the concept of the Sacred Heart was unknown." It has been shown that this statement is not correct. Several authors started collecting texts from the Fathers, but it was Hugo Rahner who brought order in this field by pointing out three themes:

1. First there are a number of patristic texts grouped around John 7:37-39, texts which speak of the living water that flows from Jesus' breast.
2. Then there is a patristic tradition about John, the beloved disciple, who rested at Jesus' breast (Jn 13:23-25).
3. In the third place there are numerous patristic texts about the genesis of the Church from Jesus' side, pierced on the cross (Jn 19:34).

I would like to develop these three themes briefly,[1] adding a further study on what the Fathers have to say about the human heart in general. In fact this last point was very well developed.

1. The patristic tradition about Jn 7:37-39

John 7:37-39 presents a problem of punctuation. The Latin Vulgate had made us familiar with a reading that made the heart of the believer the source of living water: "If any man is thirsty, let him come to me and drink. He who believes in me, as Scripture says: Out of his breast (koilia) shall flow rivers of living water." Hugo Rahner has shown that this reading originated from Origen, and was taken over by many Greek and Latin Fathers, especially by St. Ambrose and St. Augustine. Their influence has swept along the whole western tradition.

By careful research, Rahner was able to show that the older Greek Fathers favored the other reading, in which the breast of Christ is directly indicated as the source of living water, the source of the Spirit. He calls the older reading the "Ephesian" reading, in opposition to the "Alexandrian" reading of Origen. Even though the representatives of the Ephesian reading are less in number, their quality is such that Rahner is confident that he has found here the authentic reading of this passage, which is important for the study of the biblical teaching on the Sacred Heart.

A main witness for the Ephesian reading of the text is Hippolytus of Rome, who received this interpretation from St. Irenaeus, who had sat at the feet of Polycarp of Smyrna, and Polycarp had personal contact with the apostle John. St. Irenaeus:

> But the Holy Spirit is in all of us, and he is that living water, which the Lord dispenses to all who believe him in the right way. (*Adversus Haereses*, V 18,2.)

> The Church is the fountain of the living water that flows to us from the Heart of Christ. Where the Church is, there is the Spirit of God, and where the Spirit of God is, there is the Church and all grace. But the Spirit is truth. He who has no part in this Spirit, will receive no nourishment or life at the breast of our mother Church, nor can he drink of the crystal-clear spring which issues from the Body of Christ. (*Ibid.*, III 24,1.)

Another witness is St. Justin, who became a Christian in Ephesus. He has several texts referring to Jesus as the source of living water. He has even a little theology of the Sacred Heart: a combination of Jn 7:37-39 with Jn 19:34 and with the Pauline image of Christ as the water-giving rock (1 Cor 10:4):

We, Christians, are the true Israel which springs from Christ, for we are carved out of his heart (koilia) as from a rock. (*Dialogue* 135,5.)

This theology, well known in Asia Minor, is found as well in the early African Church. St. Cyprian has it, and some ancient works from Spain contain it as well:

When the people was suffering thirst in the desert, Moses struck the rock with his staff, that is with wood, and the streams of water gushed forth. In this the mystery of baptism was prefigured. For the rock is the symbol of Christ, as the Apostle says: "They drank of the spiritual rock that followed them. But the rock was Christ." No question of it then: that rock was the symbol of the flesh of our Lord, which was struck with the wood of the Cross and now dispenses living water to all who thirst. So it is written: "Streams of living water will go forth from his body."[2]

Even St. Ambrose, who elsewhere explains Jn 7:37 in the Alexandrian way, says in a beautiful prayer:

Drink of Christ, for he is the rock, from which the water springs.
Drink of Christ, for he is the fountain of life.
Drink of Christ, for he is the stream whose torrent brought joy to the city of God.
Drink of Christ, for he is Peace.
Drink of Christ, for streams of living water flow from his body.
(*Explanatio Psalmorum* 1,33.)

Here we find the expression which was so dear to the two brothers Rahner: Fons vitae, the fountain of life. Christ is the source of life, for as risen Lord he dispenses the Spirit. His Heart is the home of the Spirit, and he gives us a new heart because he gives us his Spirit.

2. *The patristic tradition about the privilege of the Apostle John*

The first to show special veneration for the Apostle John because he rested on the breast of the Lord and was permitted to drink at the source of living water was again the great Origen. I will quote, however, only one text from this tradition, from St. Gregory the Great:

> During the last supper, reposing on the bosom of the Savior, he began to drink the milk of the doctrine of "the Word," and he plunged his heart into that source of life. Like a sponge steeped in water, totally soaked in the mysteries which Christ introduced him to in an ineffable way, the Apostle appears to us a soul filled to overflowing with the gifts he has received from the Word and which he had found at their true source. (*Liber Sacramentorum: In Nativitate S. Joannis*, in PL 78,34.)

3. *The patristic tradition about the genesis of the Church from Jesus' side pierced on the Cross (Jn 19:34)*

The gift of the Sacred Heart is the Holy Spirit, obtained by Christ's sacrifice on the cross; through his blood we received the Spirit. But many Fathers interpreted the water and blood that flowed from Jesus' side in another way: as symbols of the sacraments of baptism and the eucharist, and further, as symbols of the one great sacrament, the Church.[3] As Eve came from Adam's side, so the Church, the bride of Christ, came from the side of the new Adam, when he slept on the Cross.

Already at the end of the second century Tertullian said:

> If Adam was a type of Christ, then the sleep of Adam was a type of the sleep of Christ, who slept in death, in order that through a similar cleaving of the side the true mother of the living might be formed, namely the Church. (*De Anima* 43.)

This is the second form of early Christian "devotion" to the Sacred Heart. In the first Christian millenium a large chorus of voices arises to praise the wounded side of Christ, from which the virgin mother Church came forth. This was the teaching of St. Cyril of Jerusalem in his talks to the newly baptized, and of St. John Chrysostom when he preached at Antioch:

> The lance of the soldier opened the side of Christ, and behold . . . from his wounded side Christ built the Church, as once the first mother, Eve, was formed from Adam. Hence Paul says: Of his flesh we are and of his bone. By that he means the wounded side of Jesus. As God took the rib out of Adam's side and from it formed the woman, so Christ gives us water and blood from his wounded side and forms from it the Church . . . there the slumber of Adam, here the death-sleep of Jesus. (Quoted from Stierli, *Heart of the Saviour*, p. 54.)

The sermons of St. Augustine harmonize with this universal teaching, and his words will be echoed by the mystics of the middle ages:

> Adam sleeps that Eve may be born, Christ dies that the Church may be born. While Adam sleeps, Eve is formed from his side. When Christ is dead, his side is smitten with a spear, that thence may flow sacraments to form the Church. (*Tractatus in Joannem* IX, 10.)

To conclude this section, which could be prolonged with many other quotations, let me present the conclusion of Hugo Rahner:

> The whole history of patristic teaching on the wound in Christ's side can be summed up in the single formula: Fons vitae. From St. John, who drank at the breast of our Lord, and from Justin and Irenaeus, who show us the fountain springing from the pierced Heart of Christ, a tradition of thought and writing stretches unbroken down

the centuries. It is to the deep foundation laid by this early Christian notion that the present devotion to the Sacred Heart, as expressed in the liturgy, is returning. From that beginning the development of the devotion has come full circle back to the point from which it started: the streams from the Heart of Christ, of which the prophets spoke, which Jesus promised as living water, and poured from his pierced side unto his Church, are today, as the prayer of the one, holy Church, flowing over the whole earth. (Stierli, op. cit., p. 57.)

The contributions of Hugo Rahner have been very well received. In fact, in the encyclical *Haurietis Aquas* art. 39 and 41, the patristic tradition is integrated and in art. 2 the Ephesian reading of Jn 7:37-39 is accepted.

4. The human heart in the writings of the Fathers

Generally speaking the Fathers used the word "heart" in the biblical sense: the heart is the intimate center of the person. Sometimes Greek influence is noticeable, like when Origen says that the heart is the mind; then we meet the "nous," the "mind" or "spirit" of the Greek philosophers. This topic has been researched very well by Giulio Giacometti and Piero Sessa. From their very rich collection I will quote only a few important texts.[4]

Towards the middle of the second century already, Hermas speaks of the purification of the heart:

> Purify your heart from all vanities of this world . . .
> from all doubt; put on faith, for it is strong.
> (*Pastor*, Mandatum 9, 4 + 7; also Mandatum 12, VI 4 + 5)

Clement of Alexandria (150-215) speaks about the role of faith in the transformation of the heart. In his writings, like in Origen, faith is presented as developing into "gnosis," a deep knowledge.

May this light then shine in the deepest part of man, in the heart, and may the rays of knowledge arise, to reveal and illuminate the interior man, the disciple of light, the friend of Christ. (*Cohortatio ad Gentes*, PG 8, 235.)

St. John Chrysostom has a beautiful passage on the heart of St. Paul:

I would like to see the ashes, not only of this mouth, but also of this heart, and he would not be mistaken who would call it the heart of the whole world. . . . So large was his heart that it embraced whole cities, populations, nations, for he says: "My heart has been opened to you" (2 Cor 6:11). . . . I would like to see it melting, as it burns for all who walk on the road to perdition, as it suffers the pains of giving birth . . . , as it contemplates God, for it is written that the pure of heart will see God. This heart, that was victim of expiation . . . this heart, that was higher than the heavens, wider than the world, more resplendent than the rays of the sun, more burning than fire, stronger than diamond, a heart from which streams flow . . . , where we find the source that overflows and irrigates, not the face of the earth, but the souls of men; from which not only streams flow, but also tears, day and night; that heart . . . that lived a new life; not just our life, for he himself said: "I live now not with my own life but with the life of Christ who lives in me" (Gal 2:20). Thus the heart of Christ was the heart of Paul, a tablet of the Holy Spirit, a book on grace . . . a heart that merited to love Christ as no one else loved him. (*Homily on the letter to the Romans* 32, 3; PG 60, 679-680.)

The great doctor of the heart was St. Augustine. [5] As was the case with biblical authors, the heart, for St. Augustine is not a distinct faculty but it is that deepest center of the person which is the source and term of sensory knowledge, and in which the spiritual faculties are still one. He likes to speak about the mutual penetration of memory, knowledge and love, which make the heart the image of the Trinity, an image deformed by sin and reformed by Christ in baptism. Drawing on his personal experience, St. Augustine speaks profoundly about the conversion of the heart, the purification of the heart, the custody of the heart, the anxiety of the heart, the illumination of the heart. Here I will quote only one text, about the return to the heart:

> "Rebels, return to your heart" (Is 46:8).
> Return to the heart! Why are you running away from yourselves and do you get lost away from yourselves? Why are you entering deserted ways? You are roaming around, come back! To where? To the Lord. That is too quick; first return to your heart; exiled from your own self you wander around outside; you do not know yourself, and you want to know by whom you are made! Come back, return to your heart; turn away from your body. The body is your dwelling place; the heart perceives also by means of your body, but your body does not perceive what your heart perceives. Leave your body too; return to your heart. In the body you found in one place the eyes, in another, the ears; do you find these too in your heart? Or do you not have ears in your heart? But then, why does the Lord say: "He who has ears to hear, let him hear"? Or do you not have eyes in your heart? Does the apostle not say: "May he enlighten the eyes of your heart" (Ep 1:18)? Return to the heart; see there what you can learn about God, for the image of God is there. In the interior man dwells Christ; in the interior man you are renewed after God's image; in his image come to know its maker.
>
> See how all the senses of the body report to the heart inside what they have perceived outside; see how many servants this interior emperor has, and what he can do also without his servants. The eyes convey to the heart white and black; the ears convey to the heart melodious and dissonant sounds . . . the heart itself conveys to itself the just and the unjust. Your heart both sees and hears, and it judges the other sensory data; and what the other

senses of the body cannot do, it discerns the just and the
unjust, right and wrong. (*Tractatus in Joannem* XVII;
Corpus Christianorum 36, p. 186; personal translation.)

When we return to the heart, we may learn to listen and to
see with the heart. St. Augustine tells us several times to clean
the eyes of our heart by faith, so that we may see what we
believe. The return to the heart is the first step in the return to
God for whom our heart was made: "You have made us for you,
and our heart is restless till it rests in you" (*Conf.* 1, 1).

The monks too, like Cassianus and St. Benedict, often
speak of the heart, especially of the purification of the heart
and of "compunction" of the heart, in order that we may turn
away from selfishness and sin, and that our heart may be filled
with love and contemplation. Important is a text of St. Gregory
the Great, a monk who became Pope. He stresses not only the
love of God, but also the love of neighbor, and he knew from
experience how demanding the active life can be. He shows a
way to remain in contact with the Lord in an active life:

> The holy men who find themselves obliged, by reason of
> their office, to occupy themselves with external ministry,
> always take care to seek a refuge in a secret place of their
> heart ("ad cordis secreta"); there they ascend the peak of
> their interior thought, and perceive the law as on a
> mountain top. Setting aside for a while the tumult of
> temporal activity, they meditate on God's will, on this
> summit of contemplation. (*Moralia* 23,38; PL 76,273-
> 274; personal translation.)

The theology of the Fathers about the Heart of Christ is
sometimes qualified as "objective." When they present Jesus'
Heart as the source of living water, of the sacraments, of the
Church, there is good reason to use this terminology. It cannot
be maintained, however, that they never speak of Christ's
Heart in a "subjective" way. They do speak of the wisdom and
the attitudes of Christ's Heart. In his patristic study "Devotion
to the Sacred Heart in the Fathers of the Church,"[6] Philip

Mulhern, OP, presents a section on the "Sentiments of the Heart of Jesus," in which he quotes several patristic texts about Jesus' attitudes and feelings, explicitly related to his heart: his meekness and humility, his sorrow and his joy. Two examples:

> Never did Christ sadden the weak, nor did he show any harshness even to the arrogant and the proud . . . His heart always showed itself full of sweetness and humility towards all men without exception. (Eusebius of Caesarea, *Comment. in Isaiah* XLII, PG 25, 385 D.)

And St. Augustine puts these words on the lips of Jesus in his passion:

> My heart is ready, Lord, my heart is ready. What has been done to me? A ditch has been dug for me. Even while they have prepared pot-holes for my feet, could I have done other than prepare my heart for acceptance? . . . Could my heart have done other than become ready for suffering? (*Comment. in Psalmis*, LVI, 8; PL 36,671.)

When the Fathers speak about the human heart in general, they clearly present a "subjective" theology, for they frequently describe our heart as the source of moral, religious and spiritual life. One may ask whether they also connect their theology of the Sacred Heart with their theology of our heart. [7] Certainly, this connection is not made as frequently as in the middle ages, but there are examples. We are accustomed to pray: "Make our hearts like unto Thine." But when St. John Chrysostom says that "Christ's heart was the heart of Paul," he certainly makes a connection already. And St. Augustine:

> Consider the wounds of Christ on the cross and the blood which he shed in his dying, the price he paid for your ransom. He bowed down his head to kiss you, his heart open to give you a refuge, his arms extended to embrace you, his entire body exposed as your ransom. Think of the greatness of these mysteries. Place them in the balance of

your own heart and let enter there him who for your sake
was nailed to the cross. (*De Virginitate*, PL 40, 397.)

ART. 2   THE MIDDLE AGES:
PRIVATE DEVOTION TO THE SACRED HEART

My summary of this long period is mainly based on three
important books, the ones of Joseph Stierli, Jordan Aumann,
and Giacometti/Sessa, with some reference to other sources.[8]

1. Early period of transition (1100-1250)

There was no sudden discovery of the Sacred Heart in the
middle ages, but rather a gradual and unconscious transition
from the mainly objective theology of the Fathers towards a
warm devotion for Jesus' wounded Heart, for his personal
dispositions. What resulted was a fruitful synthesis of objective and subjective aspects: the treasures of salvation from
Jesus' pierced Heart were seen as gifts of his love.

The first name to deserve mention is St. Anselm of
Canterbury, not as the father of scholasticism, but as the
mystic who summed up the new synthesis:

> The opening of the side of Christ reveals the riches of his
> love, the love of his Heart for us. (*Medit.*; PL 68, 761.)

Beside him stands St. Bernard of Clairvaux (1090-1153):

> The steel has entered into his soul. It has reached his
> Heart, so that henceforth he can carry our weakness. The
> secret of this Heart is opened by the wounds of the body
> and thence is showed to us the great sacrament of his
> goodness, the merciful bowels of our God. . . . Who can
> see anything else in these wounds? How, O Lord, could
> we see more clearly than by your wounds that you are

filled with goodness and sweetness, abounding in mercy?
(*Sermo in Canticum Canticorum*, LXI,34; PL 182, 1071-72.)

The influence of these two spread to many other theologians, especially to the Victorines, like Hugo and Richard of St. Victor. To this period belongs also the classical hymn to the Sacred Heart, "Summi Regi Cor aveto," written by the Premonstratensian, Herman Joseph.[9] This hymn not only unites the image of Jesus' corporal and wounded Heart and his "Heart" in the biblical sense, wounded by suffering love, but also moves frequently from Jesus' Heart to our hearts.

The counterpart to this hymn is formed by the first recorded vision of the Sacred Heart in the middle ages, granted to St. Lutgard of St. Trond, in Belgium (+ 1246). Though uneducated, she had been granted an understanding of the Latin Psalms, but when she questioned the value of this gift, our Lord asked her:

— "What then do you want?" She answered:
— "I want your Heart!" Then Jesus:
— "And still more do I want yours!" and our Lord exchanged the two hearts.[10]

When speaking about the human heart, in general the authors of this period use the term in the same sense as the Fathers, that is, in the biblical sense. Spiritual life in general became more affective, and the devotion to Christ's sacred humanity was further developed. This is the time in which St. Francis of Assisi introduced the Christmas crib. St. Anselm and St. Bernard speak of the custody of the heart, the Victorines about the purification of the heart. One text, from Hugo of St. Victor (1100-1141):

Our carnal heart . . . is like green wood, not yet dried from the humidity of carnal concupiscence; when it receives a spark of the fear of God or of divine love, the smoke of evil desires and of the resisting passions rises up immediately. Afterwards, the soul becomes stronger, the flame of love becomes more ardent and more clear, and soon the smoke of the passions vanishes, and the spirit is lifted up to the contemplation of the truth with a pure mind.

When, finally, by this assiduous contemplation the heart has been filled with the truth and, with all ardor, has attained the very source of supreme Truth, has been inflamed by it and has been transformed into a fire of divine love, it does not experience any more neither disturbance nor agitation. It has found tranquility and peace. (*In Ecclesiastes Hom.* 1; PL 175, 117-118.)

2. The period of the great mystics (1250-1350)

In the 12th century, the theologians handed on the patristic tradition about Jesus' Heart; in the 13th and 14th centuries, this plant grew into a tree. This development was prepared by a strong devotion for Jesus' passion, by a special love for St. John the Apostle, and by a great number of commentaries on the Canticle of Canticles. At this stage, the leading role was played by the Franciscans, the religious women of Helfta, and by the Dominicans.

a. The Franciscans

In the early middle ages, the Benedictines and the Cistercians had played the most important role in the development of the devotion; now the Friars become important.

In the story of St. Francis we are told that he received from the Crucifix of St. Damian the commission to restore the house of God. Then the text continues: "From that hour, his heart was wounded and melted at the memory of the Lord's passion." Jesus' physical Heart was wounded by the spear, and his "Heart" in the biblical sense was wounded by his desolation. The wound of his physical Heart, as we often hear in the middle ages, reveals the wound of his love. The passion of Jesus' Heart in the full sense touched the heart of Francis, who was favored with the stigmata in 1224. In keeping with the spirituality of their founder, early Franciscans had a great devotion for the Five Wounds of Christ, especially for the wound of his side.

This is very clear in St. Bonaventure, who became a herald of the mystery of Jesus' Heart, even for our days. His *The Soul's Journey to God*, truly a "Pilgrim's road-map of the heart on the way to God," shows that the only way to the Father is a burning love for the crucified Christ, and this love is perfected in a true communion of hearts. Many isolated passages in his theological works, especially in his little work *Lignum Vitae*, preach the mystery of the Lord's Heart. In his *Vitis Mystica* we read:

> The Heart of our Lord was pierced with a lance, that by
> the visible wound we might recognize the invisible love.
> The outward wound of the Heart shows the soul's wound
> of love.

More and more, the physical Heart of Christ becomes the symbol of his love; his wounded Heart becomes the symbol of his wounded love. We can catch the early Franciscan spirit again in the piety of St. Angela of Foligno and of St. Margaret of Cortona, who love to dwell in the Heart of Christ.

b. *The religious women of Helfta*

Under the direction of the abbess Gertrude of Hackeborn, sister of St. Mechtild of Hackeborn, the convent of Cistercian nuns at Helfta, in Saxony, reached the highest level of feminine culture known in the middle ages. At the same time it was a center of intense spiritual life. Among the many great women of this convent, three deserve special attention.

Mechtild of Magdeburg (+ 1285) entered Helfta late in life, after she had lived as a Beguine in Magdeburg. At the request of her confessor she recorded her visions of the Sacred

Heart, granted to her before she entered Helfta, in a book titled *The Flowing Light of the Godhead into the Soul*. One quotation:

> The Son of God appeared before me, and in his hands he held his Heart. It was more radiant than the sun and it emitted bright rays of light on all sides. My beloved Master then made me understand that all the graces that God bestows unceasingly upon mankind, issue from this same Heart. (Quoted from Aumann, op. cit., p. 61)

Mechtild sees in the Sacred Heart above all the interior life of our Lord, burning with love, to which men answer with abuse. At her entry into Helfta, she found there two young nuns who were to play important roles in the history of the devotion: St. Gertrude the Great (not to be identified with Gertrude of Hackeborn, the abbess) and St. Mechtild of Hackeborn.

Mechtild of Hackeborn (+ 1298), noble by birth and artistic by temperament, received a careful education and was entrusted with the direction of the convent-school. Our Lord favored her with many graces, but for many years she kept them hidden, confiding only in St. Gertrude and one other sister. At the command of a new abbess, these two wrote an account of Mechtild's spiritual experiences: *The Book of Special Grace*.

To Mechtild's eyes, Christ is not so much the Man of Sorrows as the glorified Lord, enthroned in the glory of heaven. Though she suffered much, she found refuge and peace in the Heart of the glorified Lord. One quotation from the first chapter of *The Book of Special Grace*:

> The Lord opened the wound of his sweet Heart and said: "Behold the greatness of my love. . . ." He united his sweet Heart with the soul's heart, and gave her all the practices of contemplation, devotion and love, and made her rich in all good. . . . After Holy Communion she longed only for the praise of God. Then the Lord gave her his divine Heart in the form of a richly decorated golden

ornament and said to her: "Through my divine Heart you will always praise me."

In the patristic period, not many texts about the human heart were explicitly related to the Heart of Christ, but in this period the two lines draw closer together. The mystics open their hearts for the Lord as the Lord opens his Heart to them. I did not find texts in which they refer their experience to the great promise of Jeremiah and Ezekiel about the new heart.

St. Mechtild also composed a manual of prayers to the Sacred Heart. They were the lifelong favorites of St. Peter Canisius, who copied some of them and carried them always with him, even on his death-bed.

St. Gertrude the Great (+ 1302), who entered Helfta at the age of five and grew up there, first as a student and then as a nun, became the greatest of the great women of this convent. Her interior life was characterized by an abundance of the most sublime graces of prayer. The treatises she wrote in German have been lost, but we still have her two Latin works, *Ambassador of Divine Love* and *Exercises of Piety*. At a later stage, these two works became widespread and had a deep influence. The keynotes of her devotion to the Sacred Heart are love, confidence and a holy joy, all penetrated with the spirit of the liturgy. The Sacred Heart was for her a school of virtue and a source of grace. The spirit of her devotion differed widely from that of St. Margaret Mary. One of her prayers reminds us of St. Francis of Assisi:

> O most loving Jesus, by thy pierced Heart I pray thee, wound my heart with that arrow of love, so that nothing of earth may abide in it any more, but that it may be filled with thy glowing love alone forever. (Quoted by K. Richstätter, op. cit., p. 105.)

c. The Dominicans

The Dominicans were outstanding in promoting the cult of the Sacred Heart in the middle ages, especially in Germany where they had 46 monasteries of men and more than 70 convents of Dominican Sisters. From the mysticism of the Passion, combined with a deep devotion to the Eucharist, they shaped an asceticism centering around the mystery of the Sacred Heart. Again, we can mention here only a few important names.

We should start with St. Albert the Great (+ 1280). In his writings we meet the Apostle John, who had drunk the treasures of divine wisdom at the Heart of our Lord. Albert returns often to the patristic idea of the birth of the Church from the opened Heart.

Outstanding too were the Rhineland mystics, among whom three Dominicans hold a prominent place: Meister Eckhart, John Tauler and Henry Suso.

Meister Eckhart (+ 1327) is the first author to speak of the Sacred Heart present in the Eucharist. In his instructions on the reception of Communion he says:

> We ought to be changed into Jesus and wholly united with him, so that all of his may be ours, and all that is ours may be his, our hearts and his, one heart.

Eckhart used the symbol of fire to describe Jesus' love for mankind, something that reminds us of the visions of St. Margaret Mary:

> On the cross his Heart was like a fire and a furnace from which flames burst forth on all sides. He was totally consumed by the fire of his love for the whole world. Therefore he drew the whole world to himself by the heat of his love. (K. Richstätter, op. cit., p. 123.)

John Tauler (+ 1361) was a student of Eckhart and was one of the greatest mystics of all times. He surpasses his teacher in references to the Sacred Heart and had much influence. A quotation:

What more could he do for us that he has not done? He has opened his very Heart to us, as the most secret chamber wherein to lead our soul, his chosen spouse. For it is his joy to be with us in silent stillness and in peaceful silence, to rest there with us. . . . He gave us his Heart all wounded that we might abide therein until we are wholly cleansed and without spot; until we are made like unto his Heart, and rendered fit and worthy to be led with him into the divine Heart of the Father. . . . He gives us his Heart wholly and entirely, that it may be our home. Therefore he desires our heart in return, that it may be his dwelling place. (K. Richstätter, op. cit., pp. 131-132.)

Blessed Henry Suso (+ 1366) was also a student of Eckhart; his spirituality centers on the sufferings of Christ in which he shared by severe austerities; still his love for our Lord, enkindled by the Sacred Heart, was tender:

Ah, Eternal Wisdom, my heart reminds you how, after the Last Supper, you went to the mountain and were covered by bloody sweat because of the anguish of your loving Heart. . . . O Lord, your Heart bore all in tender love. O Lord, your Heart, burning with love, must enkindle mine with love. (Quoted by J. Aumann, op. cit., p. 82.)

Then we should speak of St. Catherine of Siena (+ 1380), doctor of the Church, outstanding for her devotion to the Sacred Heart. She was a member of the Dominican Third Order. While meditating on the words "Create a clean heart in me, O God, and renew a right spirit within me" (Ps 51), the Lord responded by appearing to her and, opening her left side, he took her heart from her body. Some days later, the Lord gave her a new heart, saying:

See, dearest daughter, a few days ago I took your heart from you; now, in the same way, I give you my own heart. For the future, it is by it that you must live.[11]

This was certainly a privileged way to experience the fulfillment of God's promise of the new heart. What the mystics experienced in such a mystic way, God intends to do, somehow, with each one of us; our hearts are to be renewed by the Heart of Christ. In this period there are hardly any references to the Holy Spirit; the Sacred Heart is seen as the source of "grace." When we realize that the gift of Jesus' Heart is the Spirit, it becomes clearer that the Sacred Heart is the source of renewal of all mankind and of the world.

3. Expansion among the laity (1350-1700)

The golden age of medieval mysticism was followed by a decline in the 14th century. Gradually, however, things started stirring again, this time at the instigation of the Carthusians. Ludolph of Saxony wrote his *Life of Jesus*, which was to be one of the two books responsible for the conversion of St. Ignatius on his sickbed. Dionysius Ryckel, called "the Carthusian," who died at Roermond in 1471, was second only to St. Albert the Great among German theologians. As master of novices he constantly showed his disciples the way to the Heart of our Lord. A characteristic quotation of this period:

> I humbly, fervently implore you, open to me the door of your mercy and let me penetrate the wide opening of your adorable and holy side, even to the interior of your infinitely loving Heart, so that my heart may become united to your Heart by an indissoluble bond of love. (From a book by an unknown Carthusian, printed at Nüremberg in 1480.)

During the 16th century Cologne became the center of devotional life in Germany. It was here that Justus Landsberger wrote his *Pharetra divini amoris*, in which he treats at length of devotion to the Sacred Heart, and here he published St. Gertrude's *Ambassador of Divine Love* for the first time. It was by the Carthusians of Cologne that St. Peter Canisius, doctor of the Church, was introduced to this spirituality.

There follows the time of St. Francis de Sales († 1622) and St. Jane Frances de Chantal, founders of the Order of the Visitation, and many others. It is to be noted that even before the time of St. Margaret Mary, the young Society of Jesus did much to spread the devotion to the Sacred Heart. Most important among them was St. Peter Canisius, but there were many others. I would like to mention Diego Alvarez de Paz, S.J., who went to Lima in 1585. Four years later he went to Quito in Ecuador, for twelve years, and there he wrote his monumental work *La Vida Espiritual y su Perfección*, published in three volumes in Paris in 1608. This work is the first great theological treatise written in the Americas, and it contains many passages and prayers about the Sacred Heart. In Quito, Father Diego started a movement of spirituality characterized by a vigorous devotion to the Sacred Heart. This movement became a real school, with many illustrious representatives: Father Juan Diaz Camacho de Sierra, who arrived at Quito in 1623; Father José Maria Maugeri, who arrived there in 1722 and became the first great apostle of this devotion in Latin America; St. Mariana de Jesús Paredes y Flores, born at Quito in 1618 and canonized in 1950, and many others.[12]

Medieval mysticism expressed itself in prayers, poems, hymns and mystery plays. All religious societies have by now written about their contribution to this movement. Together with an increasing publicity, we find in this period also the beginnings of a liturgical cult: the feast of the Holy Lance, instituted by Pope Innocent VI in 1353; the feast of the Five Wounds, celebrated in the Dominican monasteries in Germany, already in the middle ages. The stage was set for the saint of Paray-le-Monial, who was to start the movement for the liturgical celebration of this mystery in the universal Church.

ART. 3

THE PERIOD OF SAINT MARGARET MARY (1672-1941)

The devotion to the Sacred Heart as we have personally practiced it during the first half of the 20th century and as it was practiced by the Church at large for three centuries was closely linked to the great disciple of the Sacred Heart, St. Margaret Mary Alacoque. Her request for a feast of the Sacred Heart led to a deeper study of the nature of the devotion, to magisterial documents, and eventually to a Eucharistic celebration prescribed for the whole Church.

The title "period of St. Margaret Mary" is somewhat sweeping, but I think that it is justified because of the extraordinary influence she had in this period. The Sacred Heart devotion in this period was by and large centered, not on St. Margaret Mary, but on Jesus as seen by St. Margaret Mary. There were, of course, exceptions: Richstätter, for example, centered his attention on the middle ages. But the words of Christ spoken to the saint of Paray-le-Monial: "Behold this Heart . . ." resounded in the whole Church, and met with a great response. They touched the hearts of many Christians, and even the magisterial documents, though not based on her revelations, respond to what the Lord asked from her and through her.[13]

Since the bibliography of this period is enormous,[14] I will limit myself again to an outline of the most important contributions. By way of introduction, something should be said about the French School of spirituality, even though, in time, this overlaps with the preceding period.

1. The French School

The name "the French School" is sometimes given to a movement that takes its origin in the spirituality of Cardinal de Bérulle (1575-1629).

One characteristic of the doctrine of the later de Bérulle is his view of the interior "states" ("les états") of Jesus, which constitute the depth of his soul. Though he did not often use the term "heart," he was in fact interested in what in biblical language is called "the heart," and what some of his followers later called "Jesus' interiority" (Olier) or "his Heart" (Eudes).

To understand what de Bérulle means by these "states" it is helpful to see how they relate to the "mysteries" of Jesus' life. The mysteries of Jesus' life, says de Bérulle, are past in some aspect, but they are present and eternal in some other aspects. They are past as to their happening; the Incarnation, Jesus' baptism, the crucifixion, have happened in the past. But these mysteries are eternal as to their significance. The spirit in which they were lived, his dispositions, remain actual and present in us. Our heart is called to "adhere" to Jesus' interior states; that is, we should enter into them.

Another characteristic of Berullianism is his stress on the virtue of religion: the adoration of God's majesty. In the Eucharist, we can "adhere" to Jesus' priestly attitude. With Jesus, we must learn to offer ourselves and say: "Here I am; I come to do your will."

De Bérulle founded the Oratory, and it was mainly through various members of this foundation that he had a deep and lasting influence: Charles de Condren (1588-1641); François Bourgoing (1585-1662), and two members who later founded new societies: Jean-Jacques Olier (1608-1657) and St. John Eudes (1601-1680).

Jean-Jacques Olier founded the Sulpicians, who have formed so many priests in their seminaries. He developed de Bérulle's priestly spirituality, but remained faithful to the doctrine of adherence to Jesus' interiority.

The study of the French School is important to understand the development of the devotion to the Sacred Heart. At the background of St. John Eudes, St. Margaret Mary, and many founders of new congregations, is the French School with their interest in Jesus' interiority, his attitudes, and this has been forgotten too often when the physical Heart of Jesus came to be stressed.

2. St. John Eudes (1601-1680)

John Eudes entered the Oratory of Cardinal de Bérulle in 1623. He knew de Bérulle and Condren personally, and admired them highly. He was ordained a priest in 1625 and started his ministry as a preacher of missions. His first book *La Vie et le Royaume de Jésus* (1637) was written in the spirit of de Bérulle; it was a success.

He left the Oratory in 1643, to found the Congregation of the Heart of Mary, a Congregation of priests dedicated to the Sacred Heart of Jesus and the Admirable Heart of Mary. A few years earlier he had already founded a Congregation of Sisters, the Religious of Our Lady of Charity, in 1641.

At least since 1646 he introduced in his Congregations the feast of the Heart of Mary. The text of the Mass and Office of this feast speaks also of Jesus' Heart. He stressed that the Hearts of Jesus and Mary are one. During the last eight years of his life, he started to think more explicitly about Jesus' Heart in itself. In 1672 he obtained the approval of around ten bishops for a feast of the Sacred Heart, for which feast he himself composed the text of the Mass. Pius X called him "Father, Doctor and Apostle" of the liturgical cult of the Sacred Heart.

In 1680 he completed his book *Du Coeur Admirable de la Très Sacrée Mère de Dieu (The Admirable Heart of the Most Holy Mother of God)*, his spiritual testament, for he died that same year. The book appeared in 1681. Its 12th "book" is dedicated to the study of the divine Heart of Jesus. Eudes distinguishes three Hearts in Jesus: his divine Heart, his spiritual Heart, and his corporal Heart.

We have three Hearts to adore in our Savior which, nevertheless, are but one single Heart by virtue of the hypostatic union. The first is his divine Heart existing from all eternity in the bosom of his adorable Father, which is but one Heart and one love with the love and Heart of his Father, and which, with the love and Heart of his Father, is the source of the Holy Spirit. Therefore, when he gave us his Heart, he also gave us the Heart of his Father and of his adorable Spirit. . . .

The second Heart of Jesus is his spiritual Heart, which is the will of his holy soul, a purely spiritual faculty, whose function is to love what is lovable and to hate what is hateful. . . .

The third Heart of Jesus is the Sacred Heart of his deified body, a furnace of love divine and of incomparable love for us. Since the corporal Heart is hypostatically united to the Person of the Word, it is enkindled with flames of infinite love for us. Its love is so intense that it constrains the Son of God to bear us continually in his Heart; to fix his eyes upon us; to take such a great interest in the smallest things concerning us that he verily numbers all the hairs of our head. [15]

The doctrine of St. John Eudes is a bit complicated because of his distinction of the three Hearts. De Bérulle had focused on the inner dispositions of Jesus; this becomes Jesus' spiritual Heart in Eudes. He added the corporal Heart, but does not speak of it as a symbol; he says that Jesus' three Hearts are one. This book had to wait until 1834 for a second edition.

3. St. Margaret Mary Alacoque (1647-1690)

Though Margaret Mary belonged to a moderately wealthy family, after the death of her father when she was still a small girl, she and her mother suffered very much from a dominating uncle in the house of her family. In her autobiography she wrote about this period of her youth:

I used to spend the nights, after all that, as I had spent the days — crying in front of my crucifix. There, though I did not understand it at the time, our Lord explained that his aim was the undisputed mastery of my heart, and that my earthly life would be one of suffering like his. He would become my Master just for this: to make me aware of his presence, so that I would behave as he did during his own cruel sufferings, which — he showed me — he had endured for love of me. (The effect on my soul was so deep, I would not have my sufferings cease, even for a moment.) He never left me afterwards, and I would always see him crucified or carrying his cross. In the pity and love that filled my heart, all my own troubles seemed light. Besides, I wanted to take after Jesus in his sufferings. [16]

In 1671, when she was almost twenty years old, she entered the order of the Visitation at Paray-le-Monial. Her novitiate was a time rich in grace; she made her abode in the Sacred Heart, and Jesus made it very clear to her that it was a wounded Heart in which she dwelled. Four days before her first profession our Lord told her:

Remember that the one you are going to marry is a crucified God; that is why you must become like him, and say farewell to all pleasures of life, for you will have none that are not signed with the cross. (*Vie et Oeuvres* t. I, p. 67.)

She had an extraordinary thirst for suffering for our Lord, and the Lord did send her many sufferings of various kinds, both corporal and spiritual. Shortly after her first profession the great visions began, in which our Lord revealed to her the services she was to render to the cult of his Sacred Heart. The first great apparition took place on the feast of St. John the Apostle, December 27, 1673:

He said to me: "My Heart is so inflamed with love for men, and for you in particular, that it can no longer contain within itself the flames of its ardent love, and must needs spread them by your means, and manifest itself to men and enrich them with the precious treasures that I will reveal to you. These treasures contain the

graces of salvation and sanctification necessary to draw
men out of the abyss of perdition, and I have chosen you,
as a very abyss of unworthiness and ignorance, for the
accomplishment of this great design, in order that all may
be done by me." Then he asked for my heart, which I
implored him to take, and having done so, he placed it
within his adorable Heart, showing it to me as a little
atom being consumed in a glowing furnace; and then,
withdrawing it thence like a burning flame in the shape of
a heart, he replaced it whence he had taken it, saying:
"Behold, my beloved, a precious pledge of my love,
which is inserting in your side a tiny spark of its most fiery
flames, to serve as your heart and to consume you until
your last moment. And as a sign that the great favor I have
just done you is not imaginary, but the foundation of all
those that I still have to bestow upon you, although I have
closed the wound in your side, the pain of it shall ever
remain with you; and though hitherto you have adopted
the name of my slave, I now give you that of the beloved
disciple of my Sacred Heart." (Quoted from J. Stierli,
Heart of the Saviour, pp. 115-116.)

The date of the second vision cannot be fixed any more
precisely than the year 1674. Here is Margaret Mary's
account:

This divine Heart was shown me on a throne of flames; it
was more resplendent than the sun and transparent as
crystal; it had its own adorable wound, and was surrounded by a crown of thorns, signifying the stings
caused by our sins, and there was a Cross above it,
implying that from the first moment of the incarnation the
Cross was planted in it. . . .
He showed me that the ardent desire he had of being
loved by men and of rescuing them from the path of
perdition, where Satan brings them in crowds, had made
him form the design of manifesting his Heart to them,
with all the treasures of love, of mercy, of graces, of

sanctification and salvation which it contains, in order
that he might enrich all who were willing to render to it,
and procure for it, all the love, honor and glory in their
power, with the profusion of these divine treasures of the
Heart of a God from which they spring. He told me that
this Heart was to be honored under the form of a heart of
flesh, the picture of which he wished to be exposed and
worn by me on my heart, in order to impress its love upon
my heart, and fill it with all the gifts with which his Heart
is full, and so destroy all irregular movements within it.
He said that wherever this holy picture should be exposed
to be honored, he would lavish his graces and blessings,
and that this blessing was a last effort of his love to favor
men in these latter times with a most loving redemption,
to deliver them from the thraldom of Satan, which he
intended to overthrow, that he might place us under the
gentle liberty of the dominion of his love, which he
wished to reestablish in the hearts of all those willing to
practice this devotion. (Stierli, op. cit., pp. 116-117.)

The saint continues with an account of the third vision,
which again took place in 1674:

On one occasion, whilst the Blessed Sacrament was
exposed, I felt wholly drawn within myself by an extraordinary recollection of all my senses and powers. Jesus
Christ, my gentle Master, presented himself to me, all
resplendent with glory, his five wounds shining like so
many suns. From his sacred Humanity issued flames on
all sides, especially from his adorable Breast, which
resembled a furnace, and which was open, disclosing to
me his most loving and lovable Heart, the living source of
these flames. It was then that he discovered to me the
unspeakable wonders of his pure love, and to what excess
he had gone in loving men, from whom he received only
ingratitude and neglect, "which I feel much more," he
said, "than all that I suffered in my Passion. If only they
made me some return for my love, I would think but little

of all that I have done for them, and should wish, if it were possible, to do yet more. But they have only coldness and rebuffs to give me in return for all my eagerness to do them good. Do you at least give me consolation by making up for their ingratitude as far as you are able. In the first place you will receive me in the Blessed Sacrament as often as obedience will allow you, no matter what mortifications and humiliations may result to you, but they must be regarded as pledges of my love. Moreover you will receive Holy Communion on the First Friday of each month and every Thursday night I will make you share the heavy sorrow that it was my will to feel in the Garden of Olives. This sadness will bring you, without your comprehension, to a state of agony, harder to bear than death." (Stierli, op. cit., pp. 117-118.)

The new superior of Paray-le-Monial, Mother Saumaise, to whom Margaret Mary opened her soul as well as she could, believed, on the strength of clear criteria, in the supernatural character of these visions. Still she thought it advisable to have them tested by learned theologians. Margaret submitted obediently to this examination, and our Lord sent her Father Claude de la Colombière, to whom she told everything. The Jesuit Father strengthened her on her way and assured her of the authenticity of her visions. Thus prepared she received the last and greatest revelation in which Jesus asked for a liturgical celebration of the mystery of his Heart. It took place in the octave of Corpus Christi 1675:

Revealing his divine Heart, he said: "Behold this Heart which has so loved men that it has spared nothing, even to exhausting and consuming itself, in order to give them proof of its love, and in return I receive from the greater number nothing but ingratitude, contempt, irreverence, sacrilege, and coldness in this sacrament of my love. But what I feel still more is that there are hearts consecrated to me who use me thus. Therefore I ask of thee that the First Friday after the octave of the Blessed Sacrament shall be kept as a special feast in honor of my Heart, to make reparation for all the indignities offered to it, and as a Communion day, in order to atone for the unworthy treatment it has received when exposed upon the altars." (Quoted from J. Stierli, op. cit., p. 119.)

For ten years these visions remained a secret even in her own community. In 1685 she became novice mistress, and then, slowly and with many sufferings, she was able to get the community and her spiritual directors involved in spreading this cult, though it was to be 181 years before the feast of the Sacred Heart would be approved for the whole Church.

The devotion to the Sacred Heart meant everything to St. Margaret Mary. It was her life, her spirituality. For her it meant a life in union with Jesus' loving and wounded Heart. It meant feeling what he felt, willing what was his will, loving what he loved: a life of love, union and loving reparation. To see his love, and to love him in return, that is what it meant to her.

We can, however, point out several dimensions of her loving dedication, dimensions which have influenced subsequent Church practice. I take the following summary from Bainvel (op. cit., pp. 49-69):

1. First, she put much stress on *the image* of the Sacred Heart, either just the Heart, with its flames, the crown of thorns and the cross, or the image of Jesus showing his Heart. For her the image was an important means to propagate the devotion and to get the idea of Jesus' love across.

2. Secondly, she put much stress on *the consecration* of oneself to the Sacred Heart: a complete gift of oneself to the Sacred Heart. She composed several acts of consecration herself, and exhorted others to make their own. Jesus had given her his Heart; she offered hers to him.

3. Thirdly, she stressed the importance of *reparation*. Jesus' Heart is wounded; his love is met with coldness.

She wanted to love him all the more, and express her love by suffering, penance, and communions of reparation.

Further, we should point out the eucharistic dimension of her spirituality, her stress on the Holy Hour on Thursday night, her devotion to our Lady, and finally her desire to assist the souls in purgatory.

To understand better the way our Lord wanted her to practice this devotion, especially her life of reparation, we must take into account that she belonged to a contemplative order of nuns. It was her mission to love, to pray, to suffer, to be an inspiration for the Church to love the Sacred Heart. The same spirit will lead to other expressions in active societies. We must also distinguish the devotion as practiced by the saint personally, and the devotion as she herself recommended it to others. She herself clearly lived her vocation as "victim," but she did not say that we must all offer ourselves as "victims," in the sense she understood it. It remains true, however, that we must all offer ourselves to God in the way St. Paul recommends it in Rm 12:1.

A short word about the way she uses the term "heart." She often speaks of "the divine Heart of Jesus," in a sense quite different from the one used by St. John Eudes. She also frequently speaks about her own heart, the heart that was "placed within his adorable Heart." In his study of St. Margaret Mary's spirituality, Ladame (see note 16) asks the question what "heart" meant to her. He counts 26 visions; in 19 of them Jesus presents his Heart as a sun, as a "burning furnace of love." Seven times the Heart that is shown seems to be, at first sight, the physical heart, but it is shown in a very symbolical way: surrounded with a crown of thorns, surmounted by a cross. Ladame concludes that the Heart of which the saint speaks is not Jesus' physical Heart, though later authors have thought so. The Heart that ravished the saint was Jesus' Heart in the full biblical sense, and coming to know it, she saw that it was burning with love. Of course she saw this in a "vision"; the mystery was somehow made visible. Now the natural symbol of the heart in a deep sense is the symbol of the heart of flesh, a picture of which she was to carry with her. Thus she takes the term "heart" in the sense it always had in daily language and in spiritual language, especially in the French School, but she adds the external symbol. After all, a human heart is an incarnated heart.

4. The theology of the Sacred Heart in this period

The mysticism of the Sacred Heart is marvelous; it was the delight of so many saints; it was the spirituality of so many people. But in her fourth great vision, the saint of Paray-le-Monial was ordered to work for the institution of a feast of the Sacred Heart. Enter the theologians, and the Roman Congregation of Rites. Questions have to be asked: what exactly do we worship here? What exactly do we mean when we say "the Sacred Heart of Jesus"? And what is the relationship between Jesus' Heart and his love? The theology of the Sacred Heart, though meant to be an expression of this mysticism of love, turns into a battle field.

The Sulpicians in the early 17th century celebrated a feast of the inner dispositions of Jesus, and Olier called this "interiority" of Jesus his "Heart." St. Margaret Mary stressed the external symbol as well. It so happened that the theologians who followed St. Margaret Mary insisted on Jesus' physical Heart as the object of the devotion, though they insisted equally on his love as the object. How these "two objects" were to be related was not clear to them. Froment, in 1699, speaks of the physical Heart of Jesus as the "seat" of his love. Jean de Gallifet, S.J., who as general assistant in Rome, saw an opportunity to make an appeal to the Congregation of Rites for a Mass of the Sacred Heart, presented Jesus' Heart as the organ of his love. Prosper Lambertini (later Pope Benedict XIV) saw the weakness of this thesis and opposed approval. Lambertini argued that the Church should abstain from philosophico-scientific debates about whether the physical heart of men is the organ of emotions; it would not seem prudent to approve that. And so, approval was delayed. In the meantime, the devotion continued its triumphant march in many countries, and many confraternities of the Sacred Heart were erected, with papal approval. The devotion was fully alive; its theology was in trouble.

Only in 1765, 75 years after St. Margaret Mary's death, was a theological interpretation presented that was acceptable to the Congregation of Rites: Jesus' physical Heart is the symbol of his love. Jesus' human Heart in itself shares in the adorability of his Person because of the mystery of the hypostatic union, but in this devotion we look at his human Heart as the symbol of his inner affections, especially of his love. This became standard theology.

I will bypass the endless debates with the Jansenists, especially from 1765 to 1789;[17] the promising publications and movement of the social reign of the Sacred Heart in the 19th century;[18] the foundation of so many religious congregations dedicated to the Sacred Heart,[19] and the movement of the enthronement of the Sacred Heart, propagated by Matheo Crawley-Boevey of the Picpus Fathers. I will take a quick look at some studies written during the first half of the 20th century.

In line with the ecclesiastical documents, the accepted terminology was: the physical Heart of Jesus is the material object of the devotion; Jesus' love is its formal object, for the physical Heart is worshipped as a symbol of love. The debated question was: which love of Jesus is symbolized by his human Heart? For in Jesus' love we may distinguish, first, between his love for the Father and his love for us. Against A. Vermeersch, S.J., J.V. Bainvel maintains that Jesus' Heart symbolizes also Jesus' divine love. Vermeersch lost more and more followers, though Paul Galtier, S.J. and Verheylezoon, S.J. still follow him. *Haurietis Aquas*, art. 27, solved this problem by teaching that Jesus' Heart symbolizes Jesus' love in its integrity: his divine love, his human love of God and men, and his emotional affection. The book of Bainvel, which kept growing in its various editions, was the most balanced in this period.

5. The magisterial teaching of this period

The Church documents of this period that refer to the devotion of the Sacred Heart, are so many that I will limit myself to the most important ones. [20]

1765 The Sacred Congregation of Rites, in a decree approved by Pope Clement XIII, gives permission to the bishops of Poland and to the Roman Arch-sodality of the Sacred Heart, to celebrate this feast liturgically (Mass: Miserebitur).

1794 Pius VI publishes *Auctorem Fidei*. Three of its propositions refer to the Sacred Heart devotion: it rejects the proposition that Christ's humanity, or a part of it, cannot be adored (Prop. LXI); it rejects the doctrine that the devotion to the Sacred Heart, as approved by the Holy See, is new, false or dangerous (Prop. LXII); it rejects the objection that those devoted to the Sacred Heart may be adoring Jesus' humanity, or part of it, as separated from Jesus' divinity. It states that the faithful adore the Sacred Heart as the Heart *of Jesus*, that is, as the Heart of a divine Person, to whom it inseparably belongs. This document was directed especially against the Jansenists.

1856 The Sacred Congregation of Rites, with the approval of Pope Pius IX, extended the feast of the Sacred Heart to the whole Church, to be celebrated on the Friday after Corpus Christi (Mass: Miserebitur).

1864 Margaret Mary Alacoque is beatified; she was canonized in 1920. St. John Eudes was beatified in 1909, and canonized in 1925.

1899 Pope Leo XIII publishes *Annum Sacrum.* He raises the feast of the Sacred Heart to a double of the first class, and consecrates the whole world to the Sacred Heart. The encyclical stresses Christ's Kingship over all creatures, and explains the aspect of consecration. The Litany of the Sacred Heart, which had just been approved that same year, was recommended. The Act of Consecration, published with *Annum Sacrum*, was composed by Pope Leo personally.

1925 Pope Pius XI publishes *Quas Primas*, in which he establishes the feast of Christ the King as a feast for the whole Church. On this feastday, the consecration of mankind to the Sacred Heart is to be renewed each year. The encyclical further explains Christ's Kingship: as King of our hearts, Christ must reign in individual hearts before his social kingship can be established.

1928 Pope Pius XI publishes the encyclical *Miserentissimus Redemptor.* Art. 11-36 deal with reparation: First with reparation in general: the reparation that is due to God in expiation of our sins. Christ has given satisfaction for all of us, but we should all share in his satisfaction by offering ourselves in union with him (art. 11-20). Then the encyclical treats reparation in the devotion to the Sacred Heart: a reparation offered to Christ, to console him in his personal suffering during his terrestrial life, and secondly to alleviate the suffering which Christ continues to undergo in his Mystical Body (art. 21-33).

Pope Pius XI has opened up the notion of reparation as practiced by St. Margaret Mary in two ways: First, by adding the framework of reparation in general: the expiation due to God, which is a scriptural theme. Secondly, by stressing the dimension of Christ's continued suffering in his Mystical Body, in line with Col 1:24: "It makes me happy to suffer *for you*, as I am suffering now, and in my own body to do what I can to make up for all that has still to be undergone by Christ for the sake of his body, the Church." The fact that the encyclical places reparation in this wider, scriptural context, is important, and has prepared later developments. On this occasion, the feast of the Sacred Heart was given a privileged octave, and a new text for the Mass of the Sacred Heart: Cogitationes.

1956 Pope Pius XII issues *Haurietis Aquas*, to celebrate the centennial of the extension of the feast of the Sacred Heart to the whole Church. This is the most important magisterial document on the Sacred Heart, as far as doctrine is concerned. The encyclical, in line with the previous documents, teaches that the Heart of Jesus is the symbol of love, and the nature of Jesus' love is profoundly explained. We find many new elements in this encyclical, and for this reason it belongs to the next period, where we will refer to it again. The document goes beyond the "period of St. Margaret Mary" by plunging deeply into Scripture and Tradition, and by inviting us to do likewise. Jesus becomes more and more central to the devotion, as he revealed himself to us in public revelation.

6. Pascal and Newman on the human heart

While the devotion to the Sacred Heart was making its way, people continued using the term "heart" in daily language as they had always done, and the poets continued to ponder the mysteries of the heart. Quite a few poems refer to the heart in the last verse: the poet has arrived at the deepest point.

The human heart in literature is an enormous theme; here I would like to refer to two of the most influential thinkers who have refined the notion of the heart, as current in western tradition, a tradition that starts with St. Augustine, so to speak, and of which St. Bonaventure was a great representative.

a. *Blaise Pascal (1623-1662)*

By way of introduction I would like to quote some lines from his *Pensées.*[21]

> Difference between "a geometrical mind" and "an intuitive mind" . . . Pensée 1

> People lack heart; one would not choose them as a friend. Pensée 196

> The heart has its reasons which reason does not know; one notices it in a thousand ways. I say that the heart loves universal being naturally, and it loves itself naturally according as it lets itself be moved; and it hardens itself against the one or the other as it chooses. You have rejected one and you love the other: do you love yourself by reason? Pensée 277

> The heart senses God; reason does not. That is what faith means: God accessible to the heart, not to reason (lit.: "Dieu sensible au coeur, non à raison"). Pensée 278

> We know the truth, not only by reason but also by the heart; it is by the heart that we know the first principles. Pensée 282

These few quotations illustrate that Pascal distinguishes two kinds of knowledge: abstract reasoning, and the knowledge of the heart, which is direct, intuitive and flexible. The heart of which Pascal speaks is the heart moved by grace; it is by grace that it opens itself to God. The heart guides us in our moral and religious life, and in human relationships.[22] The heart knows things intuitively, and it is not always able to express its reasons, even though it is by no means blind.

b. *John Henry Newman (1801-1890)*

On the front page of his *Grammar of Assent*, Newman wrote: "Cor ad cor loquitur." "The heart speaks to the heart."

He believes that God saves us, not by dialectics, but by
speaking to our heart.

Newman has many beautiful texts about the heart. In the
heart, he says, one finds the true reasons why one opts for a
certain style of life or for one's opinion. The gift of faith is the
answer to an innate desire that precedes Revelation. When
preaching the faith, we must discover and awaken the religious
sentiment and the principles that are hidden deep down in the
heart of the hearers, where the image of God, Legislator and
Judge, has been imprinted. Even in the hardened heart a
divine instinct remains, whereby it can always be opened to
the Truth.

The heart is the place of deep convictions. Reasons one
may give for them are secondary. The heart is the source of
knowledge because the deepest assent is the one given to first
principles, which are accepted intuitively by the heart.
Giacometti-Sessa[23] conclude that the heart in Newman is the
"synderesis" of St. Thomas: the spontaneous acceptance of the
first principles. But the heart is not limited to this function. In
the light of the first principles it also evaluates the evidence
available, in a synthetic act. In this way it determines our
options.

I think that this is in agreement, not only with the way the
authors of biblical Wisdom literature use the term, but also
with contemporary linguistic usage. Certain things we know
"deep down in our heart." Should the term "heart" in the
devotion to the Sacred Heart not be used in a deep sense?

ART. 4
TOWARDS A RENEWED PRESENTATION

Since the article of André Dérumaux: "Crise ou évolution
dans la Dévotion de Jeunes pour le Sacré-Coeur" in 1950,[24]
quite a few articles have appeared about the crisis in this
devotion in many countries,[25] and usually various contributing
factors are enumerated: the repellent pictorial representation;

the sugary and sentimental pictures; the forced language used for the prayers to the Sacred Heart; the heavy emphasis on feelings; the stress on the physical Heart; the practice of equating the Sacred Heart with the Person of Christ ("Vouchsafe, Divine Heart, to preside at our gatherings . . ."); the concentration on sins to be expiated; the dubious use of the promises made to St. Margaret Mary; the way the object of the devotion is formulated; the difficulty of consoling Jesus now in his sufferings long past, etc. Ladame thinks that the basic difficulty is a crisis of spiritual life in general.

It cannot be denied that many practices of the devotion have all but disappeared in many places. But there is also a widespread feeling that we have here something precious that should not be lost. Never were there so many national and international congresses on the Sacred Heart as during the last thirty years. Many theologians and religious agree that renewal is needed, and in this article I would like to sketch what has been contributed to this renewal. Again, I will have to be selective.

1. *The contribution of Hugo and Karl Rahner, S.J.*

The interest of these two brothers in the Sacred Heart theology was manifested by the fact that both of them wrote their doctoral dissertation on the patristic theology of Jesus' Heart and, even more, by their numerous later publications on the Sacred Heart. There is much interest in their contribution, as shown, for example, by at least two dissertations written recently on Karl Rahner's theology of the Sacred Heart. [26] In fact, their influence has been profound, though not always recognized.

I have already referred to Hugo Rahner's important contribution to patristic and biblical theology (see note 1 at the end of this chapter, and note 4 of chapter 4): he brought order in the study of the theology of the Fathers on this theme, and he gave us a new reading of Jn 7:37-38. This last contribution showed us the role of the Holy Spirit in this spirituality. Hence I should outline here the contribution of Karl Rahner to this theme, a contribution that lies in the area of speculative theology and of spirituality.

a. The notion "Sacred Heart"

The influence of the two Rahners is very profound in the first place because they deepened the very concept of the "heart." Hugo had already taken "heart" in the biblical sense, and Karl continued along this line by personal reflection. He thinks that the term "heart" does not primarily refer to the physical organ; that is already a derived meaning; there is a deeper "primal" sense:

> "Heart," taken in this primal sense, denotes that center which is the origin and kernel of everything else in the human person. It is here that the whole concrete "nature of man, as it is born, blossoms and spends itself in soul, body and spirit . . . is crystallized and set; here it is, as it were, anchored." (H. Conrad-Martius; Quoted from J. Stierli, *Heart of the Saviour*, p. 133.)

"Heart" in the primal sense, says Karl Rahner, is a primordial word ("Urwort"), like "face" or "fist," denoting realities which lie beyond the distinction of body and soul. The representation of the physical heart is used as a symbol of this personal center. We should further remember that the cult of the Sacred Heart is always directed to the Person of Jesus, but then, Jesus as seen in his deepest attitudes. These attitudes must be discovered, not by a priori definition nor by metaphysical deduction, but by a personal experience. And our ultimate discovery is that Jesus' Heart is characterized by a free, unfathomable love, which unifies all the attitudes of our Lord.

This is an important element of renewal. The theology that distinguished between the material and formal objects of the devotion failed to understand the primal meaning of "heart"; it took "heart" primarily in the physical sense, and bypassed the biblical meaning of "heart." That theology is, therefore, inadequate and dated.

For the two Rahners, the "Sacred Heart" is not just a symbol; it is the core, the personal center of our Lord. It is a hidden reality that we must come to know by personal contact. It is Jesus' Heart in this sense which is "source of life" for us. Those who reacted negatively to Karl Rahner's explanation of the "heart," mainly feared that Jesus' Heart of flesh was not given sufficient prominence. It seems to me that Karl Rahner has answered this objection satisfactorily;[27] for him, a real symbol is always a part of the thing symbolized, as tears are part of sadness. The Sacred Heart refers simultaneously to the physical Heart and to the core of Jesus' personality. In the past, the symbol and that which is symbolized were seen too much as two distinct things, and that leads to several difficulties. What we worship is the core of the Person, with the real symbol of the Heart.

Further, it is important to distinguish between the spirituality of the Heart and the devotional practices. Karl Rahner is not primarily interested in the traditional practices of the devotion, but directs our attention to the Person of Jesus. He recognizes the importance of St. Margaret Mary, but stresses that her visions must not be presented as directed against Jansenism; they are to be placed in the context of the modern situation of secularization. And since secularization has reached a culminating point in our time, this spirituality is far from dated.

b. *Trinitarian setting of the devotion*

Even though Karl Rahner focuses his attention on the Person of Jesus, he thinks the trinitarian context was lacking in the devotion as practiced since St. Margaret Mary. Christ was not seen as Mediator with the Father, so that the characteristic movement of our religion, not primarily to Christ, but rather with him and in him to the Father, was lacking. Hugo Rahner has added: we must see Jesus' Heart as the source of the Holy Spirit, who makes us love the way Christ loved. He makes us say "Abba," and moves us to love our brothers and sisters. With and through Christ, in the Spirit, to the Father: such is our religion.

c. The meaning of reparation

The trinitarian setting of the devotion is important to understanding the meaning of reparation. Karl Rahner made a short study of this topic in his important article "Some Theses on the Theology of the Devotion" (in J. Stierli, *Heart of the Saviour*, pp. 131-135).

Since in this cult we worship our Lord under the aspect of his redemptive love, this devotion must necessarily include reparation, says Karl Rahner, for it is a participation in his redemptive love, and a sharing of its fate.

> What does reparation mean in the actual economy of salvation? Sin has been overcome by the Cross of Christ, on which our Lord won his victory by a loving and obedient endurance of the consequences of sin, namely separation from God, and death. Reparation for the sins of the world, both one's own sins and other people's, must then consist primarily and essentially in a freely accepted participation in the fate of our Lord, and in bearing with faith, love and obedience, the manifestations of sin in the world: suffering, darkness, persecution, separation from God and death. (Stierli, p. 147)

The reparation of Christ as man, and of men in Christ, is offered to the Father. Our reparation is offered with Christ and through Christ, rather than to Christ. It is a sharing in Christ's redemptive suffering, and Rahner sees this suffering in the context of redemption rather than in the context of expiation and satisfaction. Karl Rahner also de-emphasizes the aspect of "consoling" our Lord, though he believes of course in the relevance of meditating on Jesus' passion. The Holy Hour, for example, is seen as a rehearsal of the believer to share in the fate of our Lord. There we discover Jesus' attitude toward the cross as the law for our own attitude towards the cross in our own life.

In his last writings Karl Rahner draws attention rather to selfless service of our neighbor, and to sharing in their struggle for justice. The social dimension started to become more important to him, but he did not integrate this in his writings on the Sacred Heart. He did treat them in his article on the unity of the love of God and the love of neighbor. [28]

2. *Haurietis Aquas, 1956*

I have mentioned this encyclical in the previous period because it is the most complete document on the devotion to the Sacred Heart that explains its nature as it had always been understood. But this document really belongs to this period of renewal, because it opens several doors. [29]

In the first place it explains the object of the devotion in a fuller way. The Sacred Heart is presented as the principal token of Jesus' threefold love: of his divine love, of his human love for the Father and for us, and also of his exquisite emotional affection (art. 27). When describing the acts of Jesus' charity, it mentions that they were guided by his perfect knowledge. Jesus' emotions are described extensively in art. 25-26. Thus the whole "core" of Jesus' personality is described. When the encyclical describes the love of Christ, the gifts of the Sacred Heart are included: the Eucharist and the priesthood (art. 36); the gift of his Mother (art. 37); the gift of his life (art. 38); the gift of the Church (art. 39); the gift of the Holy Spirit (art. 41); Jesus' continuing prayer for us (art. 44). Thus it includes the "objective theology" of the Fathers, but the gifts are explicitly presented as gifts of love.

Secondly, we must mention that the encyclical places the devotion in the light of Scripture and tradition: "For we believe that, if only the fundamental elements of this form of piety are seen in that clear light which comes from Scripture and from Tradition, Christians will be better able to 'draw water in joy' from the Savior's fountains" (art. 11). The Old and the New Testament and the Fathers are extensively quoted; the great saints of the Sacred Heart are mentioned (art. 51); the principal place among them is assigned to St. Margaret Mary. By this opening up of the authentic source of Christian Revelation, the devotion has matured. It is shown to belong to the heart of Revelation.

There are some important accents: the reference to the place of the Holy Spirit in this devotion (art. 41); the references, in passing, to "the august Trinity" (for example, in art. 11); the fact that the devotion is presented as responding to the materialism of our age, an age in which "in the hearts of many charity grows cold" (art. 68); the references to the Reign of Christ (art. 72+75); and, finally, the reference to the Immaculate Heart of Mary, to whom Pope Pius XII himself had consecrated the world in 1942 (art. 73).

The contributions of Hugo Rahner have been integrated. Generally speaking, those of Karl Rahner were not integrated, but nothing suggests that he was condemned. In fact, his doctrine can be reconciled with the encyclical, though it goes beyond it.

3. Vatican II: the need of a new heart

Vatican II does not speak often about the Sacred Heart. It is mentioned explicitly in *Gaudium et Spes* (art. 22) where it is said that Jesus loved with a human Heart. It is also mentioned in the *Declaration on Religious Freedom* (art. 11): "For Christ, who is our Master and Lord, and at the same time is meek and humble of heart, acted patiently in attracting and inviting his disciples," and in *Ad Gentes* (art. 24). In both instances, Mt 11:29 is referred to.

On two occasions the council refers to the wound in Christ's side: in the *Constitution on the Sacred Liturgy* (art. 5) and in *Lumen Gentium* (art. 3). Both texts refer to the origin of the Church. These five texts express traditional doctrine.

But what is new in the council documents in reference to our theme is the way it speaks about our hearts. The term "heart" is mentioned 119 times: five times in reference to the Heart of Christ, 114 times, roughly speaking, to our heart. Many Scripture texts about the human heart are quoted: Rm 5:5 about the love of God poured out into our hearts by the indwelling Spirit (five times); Is 61:1 "to heal the broken-hearted" (three times); Ac 4:32 "One heart and one soul" (three times). But I would like to draw attention to what the council itself has to say about the human heart.

First, there is the beautiful text about man turning to the heart. I will give a literal translation:

> For by his interiority he rises above the whole universe of mere objects: he returns to this interiority when he turns to the heart, where God who probes the heart awaits him, and where he himself decides his own destiny beneath the eyes of God. (GS 14)

Both Abbott and Flannery, the two who have published English translations, have a footnote about the Latin word "interioritas," which gave them some trouble. Flannery refers to the French word "interiorité" which the Latin text has translated literally. Both translators think that the word cannot be literally translated in English and they use a paraphrase. Flannery translates the words "For by his interiority" thus: "For by his power to know himself in the depths of his being . . ." The heart is really taken in its deep sense.

Gaudium et Spes mentions the human heart 34 times; it gives us an important message about the human heart, which I will try to synthesize. In article 10 the constitution says (quoting Abbott henceforth):

> The truth is that the imbalances under which the modern world labors are linked with that more basic imbalance rooted in the heart of man. (p. 208.)

Article 10 goes on to describe how the discords in society are rooted in the internal divisions of the human heart. Hence, to heal society, a healing of the heart is needed. This is made possible by the gift of the Holy Spirit.

> It is, finally, through the gift of the Holy Spirit, that man comes by faith to the contemplation and appreciation of the divine plan. (Art. 15, last sentence.)

Then article 16 continues:

> In the depths of his conscience, man detects a law which he does not impose upon himself, but which holds him to obedience. Always summoning him to love good and avoid evil, the voice of conscience can when necessary speak to his heart (lit.: "to the ears of his heart") more specifically: do this, shun that. For man has in his heart a law written by God. To obey it is the very dignity of man; according to it he will be judged.

> Conscience is the most secret core and sanctuary of a man. There he is alone with God, whose voice echoes in his depths. In a wonderful manner conscience reveals that law which is fulfilled by love of God and neighbor. In fidelity to conscience, Christians are joined with the rest of men in the search for truth, and for the genuine solution to the numerous problems which arise in the life of individuals and from social relationships.

When we listen together to the voice of our conscience which resounds in our heart, we can find the solution to our personal and social problems. This, however, requires an improvement in attitudes, a renewal of heart:

> This social order requires constant improvement. It must be founded on truth, built on justice, and animated by love; in freedom it should grow every day toward a more humane balance. An improvement in attitudes and widespread changes in society will have to take place if these objectives are to be gained.

God's Spirit, who with a marvelous providence directs the unfolding of time and renews the face of the earth, is not absent from this development. The ferment of the gospel, too, has aroused and continues to arouse in man's heart the irresistible requirements of his dignity. (GS art. 26.)

Article 30 specifies an aspect of the improvement in attitudes that is required: we cannot content ourselves with a merely individualistic morality; we must learn to take our social obligations seriously. The world of today needs this urgently:

> Yet there are those who, while professing grand and rather noble sentiments, nevertheless in reality live always as if they cared nothing for the needs of society. Many in various places even make light of social laws and precepts, and do not hesitate to resort to various frauds and deceptions in avoiding just taxes or other debts due to society. Others think little of certain norms of social life, for example those designed for the protection of health or laws establishing speed limits. They do not even avert to the fact that by such indifference they imperil their own life and that of others.
> Let everyone consider it his sacred obligation to count social necessities among the primary duties of modern man, and to pay heed to them. For the more unified the world becomes, the more plainly do the offices of men extend beyond particular groups and spread by degrees to the whole world. But this challenge cannot be met unless individual men and their associations cultivate in themselves the moral and social virtues, and promote them in society. Thus, with the needed help of divine grace, men who are truly new and artisans of a new humanity can be forthcoming. (GS art. 30.)

The council discovers a particular urgency of the need of social virtues at this time in which the world is becoming ever more unified. To discover what the renewal of heart means, we must also look at the needs of the situation: a new heart for a new world! We must learn to listen also to the heart of the world.

The constitution then points to Jesus' salvific plan: he brings peace and unity. He gave his life for others, and his great law for the family of God is: fraternal love (art. 32). The Church, in turn, is called to be the sacrament of unity of all mankind (art. 42), and this has implications for all of us. Governments have a great responsibility in arranging national and international peace, but the leaders of the nations depend very much on the citizens. This consideration leads to the conclusion I want to stress:

> Nevertheless, men should take heed not to entrust themselves only to the efforts of others, while remaining careless about their own attitudes. For government officials, who must simultaneously guarantee the good of their own people and promote the universal good, depend on public opinion and feelings to the greatest possible extent. It does them no good to work at building peace so long as feelings of hostility, contempt and distrust, as well as racial hatred and unbending ideologies continue to divide men and place them in opposing camps.
>
> Hence arises a surpassing need for renewed education of attitudes and for new inspiration in the area of public opinion. Those who are dedicated to the work of education, particularly of the young, or who mould public opinion, should regard as their most weighty task the effort to instruct all in sentiments of peace. Indeed, *every one of us should have a change of heart* as we regard the entire world and those tasks which we can perform in unison for the betterment of our race . . . "Behold, now is the acceptable time" for a change of heart; "behold, now is the day of salvation!" (GS art. 82, last part.)

The council makes a solemn appeal for a change of heart. The special needs of our time and international brotherhood require it. This is the most important aspect of the aggiornamento, of the renewal promoted by the council: the renewal of hearts. Structures in the Church have been changed, like the collegial structures; the liturgy has been renewed; religious life has been renewed. But all these changes are for the sake of the deepest change: the change of our hearts. God's promise to give us a new heart becomes a most urgent need.

The same conclusion is reached in the decree on Ecumenism: the conversion of the heart is nothing less than the soul of the ecumenical movement (UR art. 7+8). Unity and brotherhood in the Church require greater love, comprehension, communion.

I would like to conclude this section on Vatican II with two most appropriate quotations from Pope Paul VI:

> Greetings and peace to all the other Christian communities. . . . A cordial greeting we send . . . to those who believe in God . . . And then, at this moment, we think of the whole of humanity, moved by the love of Him who so loved the world that He gave his life for it.

> The heart assumes world dimensions; may it assume the infinite dimensions of the Heart of Christ. [30]

> To take away from the Church its qualification of "catholic" would mean to change its face, the face Christ wants and loves; it would mean to go against the ineffable intention of God who wanted to make the Church the expression of his unbounded love for mankind. We should understand the psychological and moral newness which this qualification implies.

> . . . the human heart is small; it is egoistic; it has place only for oneself and for a few others, of one's own family and of one's own caste; and when, after noble, long and arduous efforts it opens up a little, it succeeds in loving its own fatherland and its own social class, but it always seeks boundaries and limits within which it limits itself and seeks refuge. Even today, the heart of modern man finds it hard to transcend this interior confinement, and to the invitation of civil progress to widen its capacity for love of the world, it responds hesitantly and on the still

egoistic condition that it be for its own advantage. Useful-
ness and prestige govern the heart of man, not to speak of
the drive to dominate others and to use them for one's own
purposes.

But when the name "catholic" becomes an interior reality, all egoism is overcome, all class struggle develops
into full social solidarity, all nationalism is reconciled
with the good of the world community, all racism is
condemned, as all totalitarianism is unmasked in its
inhumanity; the small heart has been broken open or,
better, acquires a completely new capacity to expand. As
St. Augustine says: "Dilatentur spatia caritatis" — "Let
the space for love be widened."

A catholic heart means a heart with universal dimensions. A heart that has overcome egoism, its basic nar-
rowness that prevents man to listen to his calling towards
supreme Love. It means a magnanimous heart, an ecumenical heart, a heart capable to embrace the whole
world.

This does not make it a heart that is indifferent to the truth
of things or to sincerity of words; it does not take goodness
for weakness, nor does it confuse peace with cowardice or
apathy. It lives the marvelous synthesis of St. Paul:
"Veritatem facientes in caritate" — "Doing the truth in
love" (Ep 4:15). [31]

More than ever, our hearts must be open to all. The
universality of the Kingdom that Jesus preached, the universality of his commandment of love demand it. The world needs
it badly; the unity of the churches requires it. Our heart must
become "catholic," as the Church born from Jesus' Heart is
meant to be.

4. Towards a spirituality of the heart

The solemn words of Vatican II about the need for a new
heart were noticed by many. Since then, we have become more

aware of what is happening in many places: in Latin America, in the Philippines, in South Africa, etc. The need of a new heart became more obvious.

In this context, some started to look at the Heart of Christ in a new way: do we not find here the new heart that God promised to give us? How can we present the Heart of Christ in a way that it again means "life" for us? How are our hearts renewed by his? What is the relationship between a "new world" and the Kingdom?

It is hard to know all that happened in the more than 200 religious Congregations dedicated to the Sacred Heart but, by way of example, I would like to mention what happened in my own. In 1972, the general council of the Missionaries of the Sacred Heart published a letter in which a "spirituality of the heart" was recommended as a characteristic way of living the faith in our apostolic community. The letter suggests to take the term "heart" in the biblical sense, and to think of the Heart of God and the heart of man. The General Superior at the time, Father (now Bishop) E.J. Cuskelly, made some important contributions to such a spirituality of the heart.

In the first place, he defined the meaning of the word "spirituality": it is to be distinguished from devotional practice. A person may have various devotions, but we speak of spirituality "when a person's central intuition comes into a man's life and under its special light transforms all things else that make up the whole of his spiritual life."[32]

Secondly, Cuskelly gives us an outline of how he sees the spirituality of the heart:

> This terminology suggests several elements: it suggests that our "religion of the heart" has become interiorized and habitual. Furthermore it indicates that
>
> a. We have to go down to the depths of our own soul in a realization of our profound personal needs of life, of love and of meaning.
>
> b. We must find, through faith and reflection, the answer to our own questioning in the Heart of Christ, i.e.

in the depths of his personality, where man's yearning and God's graciousness meet in redemptive incarnation.

c. Then, fashioned by these forces, our own heart will be an understanding heart, open to, feeling for, and giving to our brothers and sisters in Christ.

d. We will not be "dis-heartened," or dis-couraged in the face of difficulties. We follow Christ who "loved with a human heart" as Vatican II reminds us; he shared our humanness that we might know that over us all is the everlasting love of the Father. In God's good time the omnipotent love of God will have its way. It is *this* love in which we have learned to believe.[33]

The next general administration continued along the same lines. They started to publish a magazine for private circulation, called *Cor Novum* and in the first issue one of the general assistants, Father Dennis Murphy, writes:

When Jesus began to preach he called for conversion, for a change of heart. He continues to do the same today. His call for a change of heart is based on God's coming to us as a Father who loves us. This love is revealed not only in the words and actions of Jesus, but particularly in his own deepest attitudes and values, that is in his "heart." These two movements of revelation and conversion take place in the heart of an individual, but of necessity they go beyond the individual too, for they change relationships between people and hence should create a new form of society. Thus there is a third movement in the teaching of Jesus — mission into the heart of the world.

These three movements (revelation, conversion and mission) do not take place in chronological order. Each implies the others and they continually interact. If anyone of them was neglected, we would be untrue to the teaching of Jesus. They sum up also what Father Chevalier saw in the Heart of Christ and what we speak of today as a "spirituality of the heart." (*Cor Novum*, no. 1, 1983, pp. 8-9.)

Subsequently, a Sacred Heart Congress was organized by the Australian province of the Missionaries of the Sacred Heart in 1985, on the theme "A new heart for a new world." The text of the conferences given was published in a book with that same title in 1986.[34] In the introduction, Father Brian Gallagher writes:

> The starting point for the congress was the passionate love of God for our world, already "poured out into our hearts by the Holy Spirit" (Rm 5:5), so that we find in our hearts a desire and a longing for the world much greater than our own hearts. All human longings, the search for God, the experiences of suffering and social oppression, the cries for justice . . . these are the concerns of a heart spirituality. The talks and workshops of the congress attempted to surface and expand these basic heart desires, believing that it is in them that we come to know God's desires.
>
> The one who knew God's desire most fully, of course, was Jesus. With Jesus, who loved with a human heart, we believe in the possibility of a new world — a new world already with us, but a new world also still to come. (pp. 7-8)

The approach of the congress, then, was to listen to basic heart desires: to listen to the Heart of Christ, and to the heart of the world, since we believe that the Spirit of God speaks to us that way too. This is clearly in line with the approach of *Gaudium et Spes.*

We must stay in touch with the longings of the human heart, with the signs of the times. And we have the revelation of God's design in the Scriptures: God's plan to create new heavens and a new earth, to give us a new heart; the revelation of the Heart of Christ and of the Kingdom. These last themes I decided to develop further in this study. The two approaches must of course go together: we have to listen to the longings of the human heart in the light of the longings of the Heart of Christ, to discover what a new heart for a new world means.

At the same time, things happened elsewhere. For several years a course was offered in the Gregorian University in Rome about the theme: "The Heart of Christ — The Heart of Man." The course consisted primarily of a study of "heart" in the Scriptures. R. Faricy, S.J. published a book on Teilhard de Chardin, [35] for whom the Heart of Christ is not merely the center of all human hearts, but even the personal Heart of the cosmos, "a fire capable to penetrate all things." According to Teilhard, the Heart of Christ energizes and personalizes all human hearts and, by the sacrament of the Eucharist, Christ makes the world his Body, by a universal transubstantiation.

Most importantly, Pope John Paul II has spoken frequently of the human heart as the center of the person from which springs everything that a person is and does. He takes the "heart" in a deep sense.

In his first encyclical, *Redemptor Hominis* art. 9, we read:

> The redemption of the world — this tremendous mystery of love in which creation is renewed — is, at its deepest root, the fullness of justice in a human heart — the Heart of the First-born Son — in order that it may become justice in the hearts of many human beings, predestined from eternity in the First-born Son to be children of God and called to grace, called to love.

In his message to the young people of France during his meeting with them in 1980 we find what is in fact a gracious example of "spirituality of the heart":

> You are also worth what your heart is worth. . . . Whatever use humans make of it, the heart — the symbol of friendship and love — has also its norms, its ethics. To make room for the heart in the harmonious construction of your personality has nothing to do with mawkishness or even sentimentality. The heart is the opening of the whole being to the existence of others, the capacity of divining them, of understanding them. Such a sensitiveness, true and deep, makes one vulnerable. That is why some

people are tempted to get rid of it by hardening one's heart. [36]

That same year he wrote the encyclical *Dives in Misericordia*, in which he presents Jesus as the Incarnation of Mercy. The love of God is a merciful love, and it is the mission of the Church to bring it to suffering mankind. The Church will only be able to do that by turning to the mystery of the Heart of Christ.

In 1986, Pope John Paul II wrote in his letter from Paray-le-Monial to the General Superior of the Jesuits, in a passage about the civilization of love:

> In contact with the Heart of Christ, the heart of man learns to know the true and only meaning of its life and destiny to understand the value of a genuinely Christian life; how to guard itself from certain perversions of the human heart, and how to join together love of God and of neighbor. This way — and this is the true reparation requested by the Heart of the Savior — it will be possible to build upon the ruins accumulated by hatred and violence, the civilization of the Heart of Christ.

The building of a new world is presented here as a work of "reparation"; even as "the true reparation requested by the Heart of the Savior." The contemplative mysticism of the saints of the Sacred Heart is becoming a spirituality fit for pastors and for people living in the world. For centuries, theologians spoke of the "natura lapsa et reparata" of man; the world shared deeply in the Fall; it is high time that it also shares in the "reparation." The Kingdom of Christ requires a civilization of love; in contact with the Heart of Christ, in contact with our suffering brothers and sisters, our heart learns its implications.

Notes

1. Hugo Rahner, S.J. developed these ideas in his doctoral dissertation: *Fons Vitae: Eine Untersuchung zur Geschichte der Christusfrommigkeit in der Urkirche*. Diss. Innsbruck 1930. Some of his later publications are relevant here: Id. "Flumina de Ventre Christi. Die patristische Auslegung von Jo 7:37-38." In *Biblica* 22 (1941), pp. 269-302; 367-403.

   Id. - "The beginnings of the Devotion in Patristic Times." in J. Stierli, *Heart of the Saviour*, NY: Herder and Herder, 1958, pp. 35-37.

   Id. - "On the Biblical Basis of the Devotion" in Stierli, *Heart of the Saviour*, pp. 13-35.
2. *Tractatus Origenis* 15 (ed. Batiffol, Paris 1900, p. 165). This work was probably composed by the Spanish bishop Gregory of Elvira.
3. Texts about this theme were collected by S. Tromp, S.J. in "De Nativitate Ecclesiae ex Corde Jesu in Cruce." *Gregorianum* 13 (1932), pp. 489-527, and, later, by Karl Rahner in his doctoral dissertation *E Latere Christi. Der Ursprung der Kirche als Zweite Eva aus der Seite Christi des zweiten Adam. Eine Untersuchung uber den typologischen Sinn von Jo 19:34*. Diss. Innsbruck 1936.
4. Giulio Giacometti - Piero Sessa, *Cuore Nuovo*. OR (Milano 1974), p. 616. This book collects texts from the whole Christian tradition about the human heart, adding short introductions. It is a very helpful source. For the patristic era see pp. 70-128.
5. For St. Augustine's philosophy of the heart see Anton Maxsein, *Philosophia Cordis bei Augustinus*. Augustinus Magister I (Paris 1954) and Pedro De La Noi, Pbro, "San Agustin, filósofo cristiano del Corazon." in Roger Vekemans, S.J. ed., *Cristologia en la Perspectiva del Corazón de Jesús*. (Bogota 1982), pp. 457-469.

   For St. Augustine's spirituality of the heart see André Godbout, A.A., *Reviens à ton Coeur*. Ed. A.R.T., Québec 1987.
6. Philip Mulhern, O.P., "Devotion to the Sacred Heart in the Fathers of the Church," in Jordan Aumann, O.P., Philip Mulhern, O.P. and Timothy O'Donnell, S.T.D. *Devotion to the Heart of Jesus*. Institute of Spirituality, Pontifical University of St. Thomas Aquinas, Rome 1982. A good book, with many quotations from the whole history of the devotion. The patristic section "Sentiments of the Heart of Jesus" is found on pp. 17-24. Henceforth I will quote this book as Aumann, *Devotion*.
7. See Philip Mulhern, O.P. in Aumann, *Devotion*, pp. 24-26.
8. Josef Stierli, "Devotion to the Sacred Heart from the end of Patristic times down to St. Margaret Mary," in J. Stierli, *Heart of the Saviour*, pp. 59-127. Giacometti-Sessa, *Cuore Nuovo*, "Il Medioevo," pp. 205-245.
9. The text of the poem "Summi Regis Cor, aveto" can be found in A. Hamon, S.J., *Histoire de la Dévotion au Sacré-Coeur*, vol. II, pp. 190-192.
10. K. Richstatter, *Illustrious Friends of the Sacred Heart*. (London 1930), p. 44.
11. Raymond of Capua, *The Life of Ste. Catherine*. (Dublin 1980), pp. 174-175, quoted from Aumann, *Devotion*, pp. 83-84.
12. See Julio Terán, S.J., "El Culto al Corazón de Jesucristo en la Evangelizació Latinoamericana" in R. Vekemans, S.J. ed., *Cristologia en la Perspectiva del Corazón de Jesús*. (Bogota 1982), pp. 470-494.
13. The year 1672 has been chosen as the beginning of this period because in that year St. John Eudes celebrated the first Mass of the Sacred Heart in his communities. The year 1941 was chosen because in that year H. Rahner published his articles in *Biblica* on the patristic understanding of John 7:37-38.
14. Some of the more characteristic books of this period, in order of appearance are:

Jean Croiset, S.J., *La Dévotion au Sacré-Coeur de Notre Seigneur Jésus Christ.* Lyon 1621. This book was written with the encouragement of St. Margaret Mary.

J. de Gallilet, S.J., *De Cultu Sacrosancti Cordis Dei ac Domini Nostri Jesu Christi.* Apud Joannem Mariam Salvioni, 1726. First French ed. of 1733: *L'excellence de la Dévotion au Coeur Adorable de Jésus-Christ.* Editio princeps: 1743.

J.J. Languet, *La Vie de la Vénérable Mère Marguerite Marie.* Paris 1729.

J. Perrone, S.J., *Praelectiones Theologicae . . . De Incarnatione.* ed. 2, Romae 1842, pp. 536-565. Perrone was the first theologian to treat the theology of the Sacred Heart in De Verbo Incarnato. He still speaks of the physical heart as the organ of love.

P. Ramière, S.J., *L'Apostolat de la Prière,* Lyon-Paris 1861. Ramière brought the Apostleship of Prayer and the Sacred Heart Devotion together, with enormous success. He founded also *The Messenger of the Sacred Heart* which now appears in 30 languages.

Jules Chevalier, M.S.C., *Le Sacré Coeur de Jésus dans ses rapports avec Marie étudié au point de vue de la théologie et de la science moderne.* Paris 1883, p. 801. Id.: *Le Sacré-Coeur de Jésus,* 4 éd. rev. et considér. augm., Paris, 1900, pp. 512.

A. Vermeersch, S.J., *Pratique et Doctrine de la Dévotion au Sacré-Coeur de Jésus.* Tournai-Bruxelles 1906.

J.V. Bainvel, *La Dévotion au Sacré-Coeur de Jésus. Doctrine-Histoire.* Paris, Beauchesne 1916; 4me ed. 1917.

L. Garriguet, *Le Sacré-Coeur de Jésus.* Paris 1920.

Paul Galtier, S.J., *Le Sacré-Coeur. Textes Pontificaux, traduits et commentés.* Paris 1936.

A. Hamon, S.J., *Histoire de la Dévotion au Sacré-Coeur,* 5 vol. Paris 1923-1940.

15. St. John Eudes, *The Sacred Heart of Jesus.* Tr. R. Flower. New York 1946, p. 51.

16. Vincent Kerns, ed. and transl., *The Autobiography of St. Margaret Mary.* London 1976, pp. 3-5.
For the life of the Saint, the first volume of A. Hamon may still well be the best, as biography. As a critical study of her spirituality I recommend Jean Ladame, *Les Faits de Paray-le-Monial.* Ed. St. Paul, Paris 1970. See further J.V. Bainvel, *La Dévotion au Sacré-Coeur de Jésus,* 4me ed., pp. 5-90; J. Stierli ed., *Heart of the Saviour,* pp. 109-122. *Vie et Oeuvres de la Bienheureuse Marguerite-Marie Alacoque.* 2 vols., Paray-le-Monial 1878.

17. J. Nouwens, M.S.C., "Le Sacré-Coeur et le Jansenisme," in *Nuove Ricerche Storiche sul Giansenismo,* Analecta Gregoriana, Roma 1954.

18. In 1882 the "Société du Règne Social de Jésus-Christ" was founded in Paray-le-Monial. This movement led to the consecration of the world to Christ the King by Pope Leo XIII.

19. Emile Bergh, S.J., "La vie religieuse au service du Sacré-Coeur," in *Cor Jesus. Commentationes in Litteras Encyclicas Pii PP. XII 'Haurietis Aquas.'* (Herder, Roma 1959) vol. II, pp. 459-498. In this article, Bergh enumerates 111 Congregations of Pontifical right, founded since the French Revolution, who mention the Sacred Heart in the name of the society; further 86 Congregations of diocesan right, and 6 Secular Institutes. Since 1959 these numbers have considerably increased.

20. The magisterial teaching on this devotion is treated by Galtier (see note 14) and by Timothy O'Donnell in Aumann, *Devotion,* pp. 165-227.

21. *Pensées de Pascal.* Teste de l'edition Brunschvicg, Paris 1930. The translation is my own.

22. For some further comment on Pascal see Giacometti-Sessa, *Cuore Nuovo,* pp. 318-327. The authors refer to two books by Romano Guardini: *Pascal,* and *The Conversion of St. Augustine.* Guardini has compared the notion "heart" in St. Augustine and in Pascal. He stresses that the heart peceives "values." A value is the preciousness of things which may not be obvious to the theoretical mind. The heart, according to Guardini, is the "organ" of

love, the love from which Plato's philosophy is born, and the Divina Commedia of Dante; the love that is "eros," an infinite desire, a spiritual hunger toward the true, the good and the beautiful. It is the "organ" of the "intuitive mind."

23. About Newman, see Giacometti-Sessa, *Cuore Nuovo*, pp. 318-327.

24. André Dérumaux, "Crise ou évolution dans la Dévotion des Jeunes pour le Sacré-Coeur" in *Le Coeur. Etudes Carmélitaines* 1950, pp. 296-326.

25. See, for example, Richard Gutzwiller, "The Opposition" in J. Stierli, *Heart of the Saviour* pp. 1-14; Jean Ladame, "Une Dévotion contestée: La raison profonde de cette crise" in Ladame, *Ce Coeur si Passionné. L'Esprit Véritable d'un Culte*. Ed. Saint-Paul, Paris 1964. Chapter 1.

26. Two dissertations written recently on K. Rahner's theology of the Sacred Heart:
Michael J. Walsh, *The Heart of Christ in the Writings of Karl Rahner: An Investigation of its Christological Foundation as an Example of the Relationship between Theology and Spirituality*. Rome, Gregorian University Press 1977.
Annice Callahan, R.S.C.T., *Karl Rahner's Spirituality of the Pierced Heart. A Reinterpretation of Devotion to the Sacred Heart*. University Press of America 1985.
Some further works of K. Rahner on this theme:
"Some theses for a Theology of Devotion to the Sacred Heart" in Stierli, op. cit., pp. 131-155, and in *Theological Investigations* 3, pp. 331-352.
"The Theological Meaning of the Veneration of the Sacred Heart" in *Theological Investigations* 7, pp. 217-228.
"The Theology of Symbol" in *Theological Investigations* 4, pp. 221-252.
"The Man with the Pierced Heart" in *Servants of the Lord*. Herder and Herder, New York 1968, pp. 107-119.

27. K. Rahner explains the place of the physical heart of Jesus in the devotion in *Cor Jesu* I, pp. 461-505, and in his conference at the Barcelona congress on the Sacred Heart in 1961, contained in *Il Cuore di Gèsu e la Teologia Cattolica*, ed. Dehoniane 1965, pp. 85-108, where he also develops his view on the meaning of symbols.

28. K. Rahner, "Reflections on the Unity of the Love of Neighbour and the Love of God" in *Theological Investigations* 5, pp. 439-459.

29. An important commentary on *Haurietis Aquas* is: *Cor Jesu. Commentationes in Litteras Encyclicas Pii PP. XII 'Haurietis Aquas,'* quas peritis collaborantibus ediderunt Augustinus Bea, S.J.; Hugo Rahner, S.J.; Henri Rondet, S.J.; Friedr. Schwendimann, S.J. Herder, Roma 1959. 2 vol.

30. Allocution of Paul VI on Holy Thursday, in *Insegnamenti di Paolo VI*, Poliglotta Vaticano 1965, vol. II, p. 210. The translation is mine.

31. Pope Paul VI, announcing the Secretariat for the Non-Christians, Pentecost 1966, in *Insegnamenti di Paolo VI*, vol. II, p. 340.

32. E.J. Cuskelly, M.S.C., *Jules Chevalier, Man with a Mission*. Casa Generalizia, Missionari del Sacro Cuore, Roma 1975, p. 104.

33. E.J. Cuskelly, M.S.C. ed., *With a Human Heart*. Chevalier Press, Kensington, Australia 1981, p. 40. See also his book *A New Heart and a New Spirit. Reflections on MSC Spirituality*. Casa Generalizia, Missionari del Sacro Cuore, Roma 1978.

34. *A New Heart for a New World. An Exploration of the Desires of God's Heart*. St. Paul Publications, Homebush N.S.W. Australia 1986.

35. Robert Faricy, S.J., *All Things in Christ. Teilhard de Chardin's Spirituality*. Collins, Fount Paperbacks 1981.

36. T.T. O'Donnell has a section on Pope John Paul II in J. Aumann, *Devotion*, pp. 215-227.

CONCLUSION

In this study I traced two traditions: a) the way Scripture and post-biblical spirituality spoke of the human heart: the purification of the heart, the custody of the heart, the illumination of the heart, the transformation of the heart by love; b) and the Sacred Heart tradition: Jesus' Heart, gentle and humble, source of living water, pierced by a lance, source of wisdom and compassionate love, source of the Church, the Heart that transforms the world by the Holy Spirit.

The two traditions come together in the moving stories of the mystics who experienced the "exchange of hearts," an experience that expresses in a mystical way something that must happen in each one of us, by an ongoing process of conversion. There is no need to stress that we are not dealing here with a "heart-transplant," but with authentic personal development. Theologians have always stressed that grace does not destroy "nature," but elevates it.

I have placed the theology of the Sacred Heart in the wider context of the promise of the new heart, and the stress of Vatican II on the need of a change of heart in view of the world situation. We need a heart open to our brothers and sisters of all nations, to our separated brethren, to the suffering and the poor. The integration of the two traditions leads to "a spirituality of the heart."

In this spirituality, the "heart" is taken as the core of the person. I suggest that also the Heart of Christ be taken in that sense. The answer to the question: "What do we worship in the cult of the Sacred Heart?" is very simple: we worship Jesus Christ in the mystery of his Heart. And if someone, in line with good scholastic procedure, insists on clarification regarding the "material and formal" object, I answer: in the cult of the Sacred Heart, Jesus Christ is the one whom we worship; the mystery of his Heart is the specific aspect of this cult.

And when we come to know his Heart, we discover its riches: Jesus' attitudes, his zeal for the Kingdom, his burning love for the Father and for us; the gift of the Spirit by whom he renews our hearts. The Sacred Heart can be symbolized, and the symbol refers to Jesus' Heart in all its depths; but the symbol is not a distinct object. Human hearts are incarnated hearts.

The cult of the Sacred Heart is part of the liturgy of the Church. The "spirituality of the heart" as presented in this study goes further. Those who want to live such a spirituality start from their own heart, with its longings and need of conversion and fulfillment. The Sacred Heart is the answer, and, renewed by Christ and his Spirit, we share in Christ's mission. For those who want to live a spirituality of the heart, the mystery of the Heart of Christ becomes central.

The spirituality of the heart is a true spirituality. It includes prayer, conversion, looking at the one whom they have pierced, listening to the Spirit. It includes love: love of the Father, care for our brothers and sisters, compassion, involvement according to our state of life. It is a spirituality of grace: we cannot give ourselves a new heart; we cannot transform the world by ourselves alone. We need Christ, we need his Spirit. Christ longs to reveal to us the plan of the Father; he longs to pour out his Spirit upon us; he wants us to share his mission, for he wants all to have life. In the Eucharist he teaches us to share bread together, and through this sacramental sharing he allows us to enter into his gift of self, into his love. We must share bread, and we must share ourselves.

The real program of renewal is the one initiated by Christ. His is an all-inclusive program, but he starts from the core of man; the rest must follow; new wine in new skins. The structures have to suit the new life; they must serve fraternity, unity and peace, among all people.

The spirituality of the heart leads to respect for people; the Spirit speaks to their heart too. To find out what they have to do, we have to listen, to learn from them the way they have to go. Their way may not be our way. Nobody has a monopoly of the Spirit. Jesus invited people to the Kingdom; he did not force them.

The struggle for the renewal of structures is sometimes hard. Just laws have to be made, and not everybody is ready for just laws. Just laws have to be observed, and not everybody is ready to observe them. I was touched when I heard in Latin America the song:

> Da nos un corazón
> grande para amar.
> Da nos un corazón
> fuerta para luchar.
>
> Give us a heart
> wide to love.
> Give us a heart
> strong to fight.

Love knows also how to fight. May our battles be always inspired by love, love for all. May the fortitude needed to fight be always that fortitude which is a gift of the Spirit.

APPENDIX

Table of the biblical texts that use the term "heart"
in the original text (leb, lebab; kardia)

The five cases that cannot pass textual criticism are put between brackets. When the term "heart" occurs more than once in a verse, the number of times it occurs is indicated between parentheses.

GENESIS		LEVITICUS	10:16
6:5	9:14	19:17	11:13
6:6	9:21	26:36	11:16
8:21 (2x)	9:35 (2x)	26:41	11:18
17:17	10:1 (2x)		13:4
18:5	10:20	NUMBERS	15:7
20:5	10:27	15:39	15:9
20:6	11:10	16:28	15:10
24:45	14:4	24:13	17:17
27:41	14:5	32:7	17:20
31:20	14:8	32:9	18:21
31:26	14:17		19:6
34:3	15:8	DEUTERONOMY	20:3
42:28	25:2	1:28	20:8 (2x)
45:26	28:3	2:30	26:16
50:21	28:29	4:9	28:28
	28:30 (2x)	4:11	28:47
	31:6 (2x)	4:29	28:65
EXODUS	35:5	4:39	28:67
4:14	35:10	5:29	29:3
4:21	35:21	6:5	29:17
7:3	35:22	6:6	29:18 (2x)
7:13	35:25	7:17	30:1
7:14	35:26	8:2	30:2
7:22	35:29	8:5	30:6 (3x)
7:23	35:34	8:14	30:10
8:11	35:35	8:17	30:14
8:15	36:1	9:4	30:17
8:28	36:2 (3x)	9:5	32:46
9:7	36:8	10:12	
9:12			

JOSHUA	17:28	10:24	6:14
2:11	17:32	11:2	6:30 (2x)
5:1	21:13	11:3	6:37
7:5	24:6	11:4 (3x)	6:38
11:20	25:25	11:9	7:10
14:7	25:31	12:26	7:11
14:8	25:36	12:27	7:16
22:5	25:37	12:33	9:1
23:14	27:1	14:8	9:23
24:23	28:5	14:10	11:16
		15:3 (2x)	12:14
JUDGES	2 SAMUEL	15:14	13:7
5:9	6:16	18:37	15:12
5:15	7:3	21:7	15:15
5:16	7:21		15:17
9:3	7:27	2 KINGS	16:9
16:15	13:20	5:26	17:6
16:17	13:28	6:11	19:3
16:18 (2x)	13:33	9:24	19:9
16:25	14:1	10:15 (3x)	20:33
18:20	15:6	10:30	22:9
19:3	15:13	10:31	24:4
19:5	17:10 (2x)	12:5	25:2
19:6	18:3 (2x)	14:10	25:19
19:8	18:14 (2x)	20:3	26:16
19:9	19:8	22:19	29:10
19:22	19:15	23:3	29:31
	19:20	23:25	29:34
RUTH	24:10		30:12
2:13		1 CHRONICLES	30:19
3:7	1 KINGS	12:18	30:22
	2:4	12:34 (2x)	31:21
1 SAMUEL	2:44	12:39 (2x)	32:6
1:8	3:6	15:29	32:25
1:13	3:9	16:10	32:26
2:1	3:12	17:2	32:31
2:35	5:9	17:19	34:27
4:13	8:17	22:7	34:31
4:20	8:18 (2x)	22:19	36:13
6:6 (2x)	8:23	28:2	
7:3 (2x)	8:38	28:9 (2x)	EZRA
9:19	8:39 (2x)	29:9	6:22
9:20	8:47	29:17 (2x)	7:10
10:9	8:48	29:18 (2x)	7:27
10:26	8:58	29:19	
12:20	8:61		NEHEMIAH
12:24	8:66	2 CHRONICLES	2:2
13:14	9:3	1:11	2:12
14:7 (2x)	9:4	6:7	3:38
16:7	10:2	6:8 (2x)	5:7

6:8	2 MACCABEES	12:2 (2x)	55:4
7:5	1:3 (2x)	13:2	55:21
9:8	1:4	13:5	57:7 (2x)
	2:3	14:1	58:2
TOBIT	3:17	15:2	61:2
2:2	5:21	16:9	62:8
4:2	15:27	17:3	62:10
4:13		19:8	64:6
4:19	JOB	19:14	64:10
6:4 (2x)	1:5	20:4	66:18
6:5	1:8	21:2	69:20
6:7	2:3	22:14	69:32
6:8	7:17	22:26	73:1
6:17	8:10	24:4	73:7
6:18	9:4	25:17	73:13
8:2	10:13	26:2	73:21
13:6	11:13	27:3	73:26 (2x)
	12:3	27:8	74:8
JUDITH	12:24	27:14	76:5
6:9	15:12	28:3	77:6
8:14	17:4	28:7 (2x)	78:8
8:27	17:11	31:12	78:18
8:28	22:22	31:24	78:37
8:29	23:16	32:11	78:72
10:16	27:6	33:11	81:12
11:10	29:13	33:15	83:5
12:16	31:7	33:21	84:2
13:4	31:9	34:18	84:5
13:19	31:27	35:25	86:11
	33:3	36:1	86:12
ESTHER	34:10	36:10	90:12
1:1 (1)	34:14?	37:4	94:15
1:10	34:34	37:15	95:8
4:17 (s)	36:5	37:31	95:10
5:1 (b)	36:13	38:8	97:11
5:2 (a)	37:1	38:10	101:2
5:9	37:24	39:3	101:4
6:6	41:16	40:11	101:5
7:5		40:12	102:4
	PSALMS	41:6	104:15 (2x)
1 MACCABEES	4:2	44:18	105:3
1:3	4:7	44:21	105:25
6:10	7:9	45:1	107:12
6:11	7:10	45:5	108:1
8:25	9:1	46:2	109:16
9:7	10:6	48:13	109:22
9:14	10:11	49:3	111:1
12:28	10:13	51:10	112:7
16:13	10:17	51:17	112:8
	11:2	53:1	119:2

19:4	48:10	63:4	31:21
19:5	48:19	65:14 (2x)	31:33
[19:6]	49:3	65:17	32:35
21:6	50:23	66:14	32:39
21:17	50:27		32:40
21:26 (2x)	50:28	JEREMIAH	32:41
22:16	51:15	3:10	44:21
22:17	51:20	3:15	48:29
22:18		3:16	48:36 (2x)
22:19	ISAIAH	3:17	48:41 (2x)
23:2	1:5	4:4	49:16
25:7	6:10 (2x)	4:9 (2x)	49:22 (2x)
25:13	7:2 (2x)	4:14	51:1
25:23	7:4	4:18	51:46
26:4	9:8	4:19 (2x)	51:50
26:5	10:7 (2x)	5:21	
26:6	10:12	5:23	LAMENTATIONS
26:28	13:7	5:24	1:20
27:6	14:13	7:24	1:22
30:16	15:5	7:31	2:18
30:22	19:1	8:18	2:19
30:23	21:4	9:13	3:21
30:27	24:7	9:25	3:33
31:26	29:13	11:8	3:41
31:28	30:29	11:20	3:65
34:5	32:4	12:3	5:15
34:6	32:6	12:11	5:17
36:21	33:18	13:10	
36:22	35:4	13:22	BARUCH
37:13	38:3	14:14	1:22
37:17	40:2	15:16	2:8
38:10	41:22	16:12	2:30
38:18	42:25	17:1	2:31
38:19	44:18	17:5	3:7 (2x)
38:20	44:19	17:9	6:19
38:26	44:20	17:10	
38:27	46:8	18:12	EZEKIEL
38:28	46:12	19:5	2:4
38:30	47:7	20:9	3:7
39:5	47:8	20:12	3:10
39:35	47:10	22:17	6:9
40:2	49:21	23:9	11:19 (3x)
40:6	51:7	23:16	11:21 (2x)
40:20	57:1	23:17	13:2
40:26	57:11	23:20	13:17
42:18	57:15	23:26 (2x)	13:22
43:20	57:17	24:7 (2x)	14:3
45:26	59:13	29:13	14:4
46:11	60:5	30:21	14:5
47:10	61:1	30:24	14:7

1 CORINTHIANS
   2:9
   4:5
   7:37 (2x)
   14:25

2 CORINTHIANS
   1:22
   2:4
   3:2
   3:3
   3:15
   4:6
   5:12
   6:11
   7:3
   8:16
   9:7

GALATIANS
   4:6

EPHESIANS
   1:18
   3:17
   4:18
   5:19
   6:5
   6:22

PHILIPPIANS
   1:7
   4:7

COLOSSIANS
   2:2
   3:15
   3:16
   3:22
   4:8

1 THESSALONIANS
   2:4
   2:17
   3:13

2 THESSALONIANS
   2:17
   3:5

1 TIMOTHY
   1:5

2 TIMOTHY
   2:22

HEBREWS
   3:8
   3:10
   3:12
   3:15
   4:7
   4:12
   8:10
   10:16
   10:22 (2x)
   13:9

JAMES
   1:26
   3:14
   4:8
   5:5
   5:8

1 PETER
   1:22
   3:4
   3:15

2 PETER
   1:19
   2:14

1 JOHN
   3:19
   3:20 (2x)
   3:21

REVELATION
   2:23
   17:17
   18:7